A Certain Loneliness

AMERICAN LIVES | *Series editor*: Tobias Wolff

SANDRA GAIL LAMBERT

A Certain Loneliness

A Memoir

University of Nebraska Press | Lincoln and London

Acknowledgments for the use of copyrighted
material appear on pages 193–94, which consti-
tute an extension of the copyright page.

Publication of this volume was assisted by a
grant from the Friends of the University of
Nebraska Press.

Library of Congress
Cataloging-in-Publication Data
Names: Lambert, Sandra Gail, author.
Title: A certain loneliness: a memoir /
Sandra Gail Lambert.
Description: Lincoln: University of Nebraska
Press, 2018. | Series: American lives
Identifiers: LCCN 2017049907
ISBN 9781496207197 (pbk.: alk. paper)
ISBN 9781496208620 (epub)
ISBN 9781496208637 (mobi)
ISBN 9781496208644 (web)
Subjects: LCSH: Lambert, Sandra Gail, author. |
Women authors, American—Biography. |
Loneliness. | Isolation.
Classification: LCC PS3612.A54648 Z46 2018 |
DDC 813/.6 [B]—dc23 LC record available at
https://lccn.loc.gov/2017049907

Set in Fanwood Text by E. Cuddy.
Designed by L. Auten.

WOMAN VS. HERSELF

Her skin is cold
and damp as a window.

She looks at herself in the glass
and thinks *Yes*

I have that to give.

Sun diminishes
frost on the pane

Outside, the sound of ice.

REBECCA LINDENBERG, *Love, an Index*

CONTENTS

Acknowledgments   ix

Solace: Three of
the Places   1

The Laundromat   3

Figuring It Out   7

Well-Nourished
White Child   13

Atlanta—1968   19

Sex Objects   21

Complex Math   25

Atlanta—1984   29

Becoming Lazy   31

Rolling in
the Mud   37

Open-Water
Swimmers   45

Pass the Hemlock   49

Poster Children   59

The Art of
Budgeting   65

Mosquitoes   69

Negotiating a Life   83

Dehiscence   91

May or May Not   99

Atlanta—2007   105

The Last Period   107

Immoderation
and Excess   117

Looking for the V   119

Yielding   133

I Am Here, in This
Morning Light   141

Pride Goeth   157

Horror in the
Okefenokee   163

I'm Fine,
Thank You   165

The Blind Girl
and the Cripple
Get on a Plane   169

The Swimmer   185

*Source
Acknowledgments*   193

Thank you. Thank you to the staff and supporters and imaginers of artist retreats and residencies. Yaddo, the Studios of Key West, and the Atlantic Center for the Arts provided support in the writing of this memoir. Thank you to the creators of the literary journals and anthologies who accepted my writings. They are listed in the back. And thank you to Alicia Christensen and everyone else at the University of Nebraska Press for including my memoir in the American Lives Series.

Much of the writing was done camping in Florida's state parks, parks that continue to exist and remain glorious because of the efforts of rangers, volunteers, and environmental activists. There is a motel in the small fishing village of Cedar Key where I would retreat a few times a year and where the front office and housekeeping crew made it possible for me to write productively. Many writers have helped me. Sarah Einstein, Aliesa Zoecklein, and Michele Leavitt's unwavering belief in my writing (and mine in theirs) continues to fortify, comfort, and sustain.

One day I was deep in revision of this memoir. It was a difficult section, one without much hope. So I took a Facebook break. And there was that smokin' hot woman who had been "liking" a lot of my posts. I tapped my finger on the manuscript pages beside me. "You know," I said to myself, "you could maybe change this." And so I contacted the smokin' hot woman. Which means that now I get to thank my wife, Pam Paris, for her unconditional and wildly enthusiastic championship of my work.

A Certain Loneliness

Solace

Three of the Places

I called them ladies-of-the-valley. In 1960 we lived in Norway, and down the hill from our house was a forest. It seemed so very far away. It probably wasn't, since I was only six. Deep in the woods was a place the sun reached through to the ground, and at the edges of the light, in its shadow, the flowers spread over the forest floor. I'd sit among them and smooth the skirt of my dress around me. The bare skin between my panties and the top thigh band of my braces pressed into the wet slickness of the ground. The white pearls of flowers about to open would perch on my fingertips, and they seemed to have no weight. Cars, construction, my mother's voice, and the confusions of where to sit on the school bus or why no one sat with me and the relief of reaching the classroom and the kindness of the teacher also lost any substance. The honey perfume of the disturbed plants rose around me.

It turns out that lily of the valley and all of its parts—stems, roots, flowers, leaves—are poisonous. It slows the heart.

Three years later the woods, which by then I thought of as nothing but an empty lot (and now know were a remnant of massive virgin forest), were cleared. But there was still the hill behind my house too steep to build on. I'd walk up it as far as possible and then drop my crutches and scramble with my hands to the top where I'd sit among pine needles and low-bush blueberries. I'd reach and reach until I ate a circumference of berries. From there, through trees, was a view of mountains in a blue mist. The muscles around my eyes rearranged themselves, and I could focus into a far distance. When I was young I thought that seeing far away, like through a telescope pointed at the stars, would let me see into the future. Now I know that telescopes show us the past. They show us the light of stars long after the star itself has exploded and gone dark.

When I was thirteen I could name a lot of what I needed relief from. Not being allowed to stay up and watch television programs the rest of my classmates watched, the pain of the contraption put on my legs at night that was supposed to untwist my bones, a tattletaling little sister: I could describe these affronts at great length and with the unrelenting harshness of a teenager, but only in my head. I was considered almost too old for a spanking, but not quite. A door slammed in reaction to parental intransigence, or a poorly timed and so overheard screaming argument with my sister could still lead to the quick rattle of a buckle, the slick sound of a belt pulled through loops, a humiliation. I had learned to be careful. And I had learned the comfort of stolen alcohol. But also, sometimes, in our front yard, a deep winter sun would slant through the grove of silver birch. The ice coating the limbs exploded in light. The white of the trunks became translucent, and I'd put my hand out and imagine it sinking through the bark.

The Laundromat

"You are so inspiring."

In my experience, it's impossible to shut them down once they start, but I try. With each hand gripping a rim, I make a hard spin toward my last dryer. I open the glass door and angle the wheelchair close. It reassures me that, except for the rhinestone glasses, the woman appears to be my age and therefore can't have any crippled-up grandchild to talk about. Just in case, I put my head deep into the drum.

I'm in my late thirties now and for all my laundromat years I've known never to smile at anyone or to catch an eye, but these days I'm using a wheelchair instead of braces and crutches. Physically, the laundromat should be easier, since I can carry big loads in and out on my lap, and it's 1988, so places are starting to have ramps. But the wheelchair also means a whole new barrage of comments. I've delayed doing a wash until my sheets are gray and a rash has spread under my breasts, maybe from the sheets but most likely because of the towels. No one comes into my bathroom or my bed but me, so no one knows, so I can live this way. But now my work clothes, after rewearings and despite strategic spot washes, have become unacceptable.

"Really, so amazing." The voice is directly behind me. I wedge farther into the dryer and pretend to retrieve a sock. It's steamy, dark, and quiet—until the woman's voice echoes around my head.

"My niece, poor thing—it's a tragedy for her parents really. She's afflicted like you. It's a miracle the way you do for yourself like this, and I'm going to tell them I saw you. It'll give them a little hope. Now my brother's wife, she's a saint."

There's a mute button in my head for these moments. I push it. I grab a towel and plop myself out of the dryer and onto the wheelchair seat. The towel is flecked with bits of tissue. I pick at them. The woman's mouth is still moving. Her glasses sparkle as they move closer. Her eyes reflect in the bright, watery way I've come to associate with the overly religious. They, more than most in my experience, lack the ability to notice social cues that tell them to shut up and go away, far away. Her lips have an unctuous sheen. I'm in anticipation of having my head patted. I'll listen forever, but they don't get to touch me.

"But I always say, God doesn't—." The monologue stumbles as I snap the towel out between us. Twice. It cracks at the woman's chest. "Oh look, my machine has stopped. Honey, I'll be right over there if you need any help."

Now that the confrontation is over, I reach for more laundry. Next out is a handful of underwear. I fold each one into careful thirds and avoid snagging a nail on the lace or black silk twisted among the cotton. My mind wanders around the thought of not wearing underwear anymore. Now that I use a wheelchair they're a hassle to pull up and down and sort out under my pants. But the silky ones caress my thighs the way water does when I swim. Just those, I decide, I'll keep. And a cotton pair for doctor visits. The others can be thrown away. And again, as I figure out another, easier way to live with this new wheelchair, my lungs leap as if they can expand all the way into my shoulders. My spine lifts as well, and the word *liberation* comes to mind.

My head is jerked forward as two arms snake around my neck, overlap on my chest, and squeeze. "Jesus loves you" comes a whisper in my ear, and the moistness of the woman's breath drips onto my neck. The world contracts—I contract—to just the space between her arms. It's as if there's no air. I gasp and pull at the arms on my chest. They tighten in response. I try to yell, but my breath is too ragged. I'm sure I'm suffocating. One of the arms is near my teeth.

I do not bite through the flesh down to the bone. Instead, I imagine the far horizon of a prairie and the rush of air just before a thunderstorm, and I'm able to inhale past the pressure, and I can see more than the puckering of skin around the erect hairs on an arm, and this woman can no longer diminish me. So I don't bite her. But she is assaulting me. I grab a deeper breath despite the way it stinks of her and sink my nails into both of the soft forearms hard enough to hurt. I'm careful not to break the skin. I'd go from "inspiring" to "she attacked me, officer" pretty quick. The woman tries to escape, but I hold on and turn my head to bring our faces close.

"Fuck you, bitch, and fuck Jesus. Touch me again and I'll call the cops." I let go, and the arms whip back. Footsteps rush away. I pull my shirt away from my body. It's damp where the woman touched me. Why are these people always sweaty? I wipe my neck dry with the clean underwear before I lob them into the trash bin. At least *fuck* is still the magic word for her type. Past combinations of *damn Jesus, screw Jesus,* or a *fuck off* without the Jesus have been less effective repellents.

Deep in the dryer I find a still-hot towel. It burns as I use both hands to press it hard against my chest. The heat seeps in around my heart. I breathe the faint flower perfume of old dryer sheets.

Figuring It Out

My nine-year-old wrinkled fingers gripped over the edge of the pool, and I leaned my head back to gasp with effort and with triumph. I'd swum farther than I ever had. My coach's bare feet stepped between my hands. Through a smear of chlorine rainbows I could see stout calves and then hair that thickened up thighs and curled around the crotch of a gray, utilitarian bathing suit. She leaned over, and echoes bounced off the tiled walls as she yelled into my water-muffled ears. I lip read *veldig bra* and *en gang til*—Norwegian for "very good" and "one more time." This adult, unlike so many others in my life, never said something was good unless it had been. I didn't think I had any strength left, but she wanted more, so I imagined myself a dolphin leaping as I pushed against the wall and twisted. The muscles that moved my arms through the water sang to me, to my breath, and I stroked until my body rode the surface and momentum was restored.

When she decided we were done, I sat with bent-over shoulders on the side of the pool and gulped steamy air in a thrill of well-earned exhaustion. I'd figured out when to breathe, my hand hardly splashed at all coming down into the water, and I'd swum forever. My coach squatted beside me and allowed that I might be ready to learn the butterfly. I was as happy as a serious little girl ever got.

I shouldn't have been there according to the doctors at the military hospital. They said my spine was too curved for exercise and then put me in a plastic corset. They agreed with my doctor at the Warm Springs Polio Foundation that as soon as the Air Force reassigned us back to the States, I should have surgery to insert steel rods and then be flat in bed for six months. The last set of surgeries had been on my legs when I was five, which was almost half my life ago. Only blurred memories remained, but as the doctors talked, my body contracted and folded in on itself. My arms had wrapped around my knees in protection and comfort.

Norway had socialized medicine, so my parents thought why not make an appointment. This doctor said I needed to be stronger or things would get worse. Get rid of the corset, he said. How about swimming, he suggested. They had a program. Already I'd learned to worry about patronizing volunteers with their syrupy voices, but this woman, who was now telling me that I'd done well but that next time I'd do better, who lifted me up in her arms and carried me to the showers, she was a retired Olympic swim team coach. And I was one of her athletes.

Norwegians believe that in the winter, after a warm swim, one must close the body's pores. A quick, naked roll outside in the snow is acceptable, but we were in downtown Oslo, so it was the showers instead. My coach reminded me that this was part of the training and shifted me over her hip to reach for the faucet. I closed my eyes. My breath stopped with the first groan of the pipes. They knocked and shook until a spurt and then a full flow of cold-thickened water hit my back. She rotated us twice, and it was over. Once again, I'd endured. A sense of worthiness lifted my head over the coach's shoulders as she carried me to a bench.

She left me there with my clothes, towel, leg braces, and crutches. All around women wandered naked except for their shower caps. My coach stripped off her bathing suit and chatted with friends, their bodies loose and easy in the damp heat. Even though I put on an undershirt before taking off my suit and hunched long johns over my rear end right away, and no one spoke to me, I felt accepted. One at a time, I positioned a leg brace on the bench while I watched these women through my lowered eyelashes. Bare thighs moved in and then out of my field of view and flexed their wet muscles and rose into a thickness of hair. I slid my legs between the braces' aluminum rods until the top edges tucked into my groin. I lifted my feet into the attached saddle oxfords and paused to stare without staring at a woman reaching for her bra. For a moment the bottom curve of a breast lifted into view. I belonged because I was a swimmer, a good swimmer, maybe better than some of them, and because of the knowing that comes before knowing when you grow up to find a home in women's bodies.

I tightened and tied shoelaces and buckled the sweat-softened leather straps over my knees and around my thighs. In a long forward stretch, I maneuvered the waistband of my pants around the shoes and worked the fabric over all the places it caught on the way up. I was seal skin–booted, wool-mittened, and had my down parka zipped before I fit my arms into the crutches and used my hips to kick both legs straight. The spring-loaded knee locks snapped into place as I stood.

At the exit to the outside, my shoulder pushed at the thick door until I could wedge it partway open with a crutch tip. With a practiced sideways step, I rotated my body around the crutch and was through the space just as my arm pulled out of the way. The door slammed shut a breath of an inch from my knuckles. It had become a sport to execute this maneuver in as showy a way as possible.

Our family station wagon idled at the curb with steam swirling out of the tailpipe. My father made a blurred gesture at me from behind the frosted window, but I paused in the entranceway. The skin around my eyes tightened, and my lips puckered as the cold froze each molecule of moisture in my exposed face. I felt clean. The window of the car rolled down, and cigar smoke roiled into the air.

"Anytime."

The window rolled back up.

My father understood discipline and accomplishment. He would be impressed with my new number of laps. It would be a good ride home. My shoulders pitched forward, and the easy strength of my arms swung my body through the crutches. The joy of those moments between the building and the car was that I knew who I was. I was a swimmer. I tucked my chin and smiled. Ice crystals shattered and crackled around my mouth, over my cheeks, and along my temples.

The Air Force moved us back to the States, and there were no pools to swim in. My parents said that everything cost too much, and everywhere was a long drive. Swimming dropped out of my life. My mother signed me up for the Girl Scouts. It had never been easy for me to join in with groups, but I earned badge after badge, more than anyone else, until my sash was heavy with them. I was smug about this. The other girls made sure I found out that the troop leaders were dumbing down the requirements for me, even the nonphysical ones, like how many books for the reading badge. I threw out the sash. I told my mother I'd lost it. I told my mother I just didn't want to go anymore. I missed my coach with her sparse, overearned praise.

We returned to the surgeon at the Warm Springs Polio Foundation, who yelled at his nurse and called her incompetent and useless and some other word I wasn't sure of. He told her to go back and get the right X-rays this time. My mother moved closer to the door, I shrunk low on the exam table, and my father sat to attention. But the nurse stepped up to the light box, hit her finger against my name at the bottom, and glared at the doctor. The doctor peered at the nameplate above her fingernail. He slapped an older X-ray up beside the first. He looked from one to the other and then sat back and gave us the good news. My spine, the dangerous upper part of the curve, had straightened, and no surgeries were required.

Well-Nourished White Child

I read the old hospital chart. "Well nourished, white, three years nine months old. Previous surgical procedures on left hip, left knee, and left heel cord." I don't remember the child. I know from my mother there were two surgeries and two body casts. I don't remember that I lay by myself, covered in plaster from chest to knees, on bleached sheets in a small, windowless room at the end of a hall, but my mother tells me it was so.

The child looked at green walls through the rails on a metal bed. I've seen a photo, although I've made up that the walls were green. There must have been a chair, an overhead fluorescent light, and a sink in the corner with a shelf that stored ointments and hard soap. I can almost remember a metal trashcan with a lid that clanged shut over an encrusted bandage or dirty diaper.

The child listened to the noises around her; her life depended on it. She must have strained to hear the muffled sounds outside the heavy door: distant bells, elevator doors opening and closing, and the rattle of food carts three times a day. My body still startles at the leap in volume when a door is pushed open. I don't remember the smell of yellowed wax on linoleum, a nurse's perfume, or the shameful ammonia of urine. Sometimes, in the middle of a menopausal hot flash, I think I remember the clamminess that matted the hair along the back of the child's neck into knots that my mother said had to be cut out. How did the child pass her days? She couldn't read yet, and there was no television. I'm going to say that she had a stuffed animal, a bunny, and it was soft. She told stories to her bunny and pulled the sheet over their heads to play house, to make a home for them.

Sometimes, in my dreams, I hear the clicking of high heels. They are always early dawn dreams that I can't fully recall but wake from full of tears. I've imagined a story to go with the sound. In 1956 hospitals allow the mother to visit for one hour a day. In my story the child can see beyond the door of her room and into the hall. The elevator doors ding open, and her young mother walks off, stilettos sharp against the floor. Her mother pauses at the nurse's station and rests one hand, with its perfection of ruby red nails, on the counter. She asks for an update. She continues down the hallway but pauses outside the room. Light falls across her daughter's face when she eventually opens the door.

I know how the story ends. My mother has told me. Each day, when the hour was done, the child screamed and begged her mother not to go. The mother heard the screams even on the elevator after the doors closed. But in the hour before, did the mother read about ugly ducklings and engines that could? Was there a place between skin and plaster where she could fit her hand? Did those fingernails reach under the cast and scratch the itchy, damp skin? Did the child moan from the pleasure of it?

The light lifted off the snow as bright as daytime but blue and thin. I left my crutches at the side of the road, dropped to sitting, and pushed off the edge. My body rolled and slipped, and when I ended up face forward, I put my arms out in front like runners, and it was as if I were my own sled. The speed was the wondrous kind of scary that leaves a twelve-year-old sure she has power in the world. As the momentum slowed, I was left far out in the middle of a white field. I turned face up and lay there, arms spread, suspended over the surface except where the weight of my leg braces pushed into the snow. The dark pines threw moon shadows over me.

The ski lodge seemed far away. I'd spent another day inside, alone. Through the yard that morning I heard the shout of a husband asking his wife to find a lost glove, the snap of boots kicked into their bindings, and the back and forth hiss of waxed skis being tested. Everyone but me strode forward across the mountain. I read from my stack of books, made a sandwich, napped, and read again. First the weakest skiers returned, and then the couple who had dinner duty, and finally the most skilled skiers. Sound returned as well: boots on the staircases, a shouted challenge to a Yahtzee game, my sister invading the room, the clang and whistle of steam rising into radiators.

This night, like the other nights, all of the families vacationing on this mountain in Norway were having the evening's cocoa or brandy. They were rubbing their bellies and thanking the cooks. They were telling stories of the day's dramatic falls, a broken pole, the miles covered, and they were laughing and showing off goggle-shaped sunburns. No one would miss me.

This white world in the field was silent and perfect. I was perfect. Time vanished. Had I been here forever? Could I stay here forever? The cold seeped through wool and goose down and spread along my spine until I twisted onto my side. As I pushed against the snow to try to sit up, my arm sank past my shoulder until my cheek pressed into the snow. I angled an eye up until it ached but still couldn't see to the top of what had been a gentle slope on the slide down. My breath melted the snow around my chin with each exhale, and with each inhale the snow refroze into a crystal sheen. I rolled onto my stomach and pulled forward. My strong arms sank again and again.

With both arms buried and sweat chilling under my clothes, I stopped moving.

I was good at figuring things out on my own. I had been for a long time. This pride laid itself like a favorite blanket over the panic of no one knowing where I was, of no one looking for me, of a little kid in the hospital and her useless crying for pain relief, for help peeing, just because. My shoulders rocked, and deep in the snow my arms shifted until they could pull free. They spread themselves flat over the snow. I wiggled and muscled and elbowed up the hill and stopped only when one hand hit metal and gripped onto the center post of my crutch. Using it for support, I got on my knees, spread both crutches wide, shoved my arms against the cuffs that cradled my biceps, and braced the rubber tips deep into the snow. My breath slowed as I concentrated my strength. My body lifted until it was standing. The lights of the lodge came back into view.

The snow on the road groaned under my feet as I walked back to the lodge. I had learned to push my crutches hard into the snow two times, making a wedge before I swung my weight through. The way each crutch pushed against my grip told me how wide a stride I could risk—wider if there was a crust and narrower if the snow was powder over ice. Sometimes trucks came by and spread gravel, which made the terrain uncertain, and I'd keep my crutches tucked underneath me, unwilling to trust them for anything but light support and balance as I shuffled my feet forward. Tonight there was a packed, thick snow that grabbed my crutch tips and held them steady. But I didn't swing far. The smaller steps kept my crutches from slipping backward.

It didn't take long until I could hear the music. By now my mother was among the singing group swaying close around the piano bench as the husband of the wife who drank the most played and led the songs. Closer to the fire my father would be sitting in a leather chair. At least twice during the week of our vacation, someone told the joke about my father, about how when he tumbled down a mountainside, ski poles flailing, he always stood back up with his cigar still in his mouth and still lit.

A lover stops touching me or perhaps it's me who doesn't touch her. We're not apart yet. We still make love, but our arms don't curl together in movie theaters, and neither of us makes the effort to lean over the side of my wheelchair to caress a wrist, fix a collar, or place a hand on the other's cheek. As touch becomes occasional (an occasion) for a short, precious while, I rage. It's a private tantrum that has nothing to do with the "why can't you ever . . ." accusations or arguments over "who appreciates who enough." It's about what I know comes next as the stages of dissolution jerk onward and separation becomes a relief.

A containment will travel from the surface of my body down through thin fibers and membranes of connective tissue. It will spread among a swirl of sweat and sebaceous glands and blood and lymphatic vessels. It will stiffen the nerve endings that allow me to feel touch and heat. The system will recalibrate. The craving for physical connection, the comfort of it, the urging it provides toward emotional intimacy contracts, is lost, becomes repellent. A serene, almost formal reserve then becomes the norm. Only drinking will diminish it enough to allow for liquid, blurred, random sex. I don't know how to stop this hardening.

I resist. I am a person. I say this out loud in my empty bedroom and hear how defensive it sounds, how lacking in any pride. I try again. It is my right to be engaged in the messy human condition of love. And now my voice is shrill and demanding. Fuck, just fuck. This last is said with such sadness, as all the anger and bitterness I can hold are smothered and then forgotten. In my mind and within my cells, the new order will seem right. Not good—but right, as if I've always been physically alone. Each morning I'll wake and stretch my arms over into the far, cool, unwrinkled expanse of sheet until all I know is that this is how the world is, how I am, how it was, always was, and ever will be.

Atlanta–1968

My family has driven in from the suburbs. Our station wagon is traveling down Ponce de Leon Avenue, and we're in the standard nuclear family seating configuration. My younger sister leans forward between the seats to talk to my parents. I'm pressed against the side door with my body turned to the window. Atlanta scenes go by—liquor stores, shops with bars on the windows, and sidewalks with black and white people walking on them. It's dusk, and streetlights are turning on. I'm fifteen years old.

We stop at the traffic light just past the Sears store. Outside my window is a low building with faded yellow paint and its few windows blacked out. There's a door with a dim light under the overhang. A person stands to one side of the door leaning against the wall and smoking. She, I know it is a she, is stocky, muscular, and wears men's work clothes. I can't stop staring. I want to go to her, lean up against her, be inside that building. My yearning has no words.

The light changes, and my father drives on.

Sex Object

The skirt was a 1966 home economics class project. The hem ended up uneven, the waistband was a joke, and the pattern of green and black checks stretched into fun house mirror waves over my hips. It was too tight. But I liked that. I liked the press along my belly. I liked how I had to wiggle the skirt down my legs when it rode up.

A pack of girlfriends had snuck into an over-eighteen event. All of us wanted to face the dance floor, so we crowded our chairs together at a table and waited. The waitress placed our beers in a semicircle in front of us. We pretended to talk to each other, but mostly we peeked beyond our glass fencing to notice if anyone, any man, was looking at us or walking close or might ask us to dance.

Soon one of them approached. He wasn't old, wasn't creepy, and had a blush on his cheeks. We all had individual, awkward, fourteen-year-old reactions. One of us stared straight at him and smiled big. Another pulled a strand of hair over one eye, pushed it behind an ear, pulled it over her eye again. Another kept her head turned and fake-talked with another of us who was holding her breath. As soon as he got close, I looked to the side of him, so I wouldn't have to see when I wasn't chosen. I was never chosen.

The staring-straight-at-him girl tapped my arm, then tapped again harder, then dug her fingernails in. I refocused from my practiced long stare and mouthed "ow" at her. She stared at me, and then her eyes darted toward the dance floor, toward the boy.

I looked at him. He had his hand out. He asked if I would dance with him. He shifted his weight from side to side and had to gulp halfway through the short sentence. His uncertainty satisfied a just-that-moment-discovered need inside me. The hot thrill of sexual power lit up my skin, stretched my shoulders back, and jutted my breasts even farther out over the table.

I nodded to him. And then I had to look away in order to gather up my crutches from where they were lying on the floor. I slapped my arms into them, lifted myself to standing and kicked out first one leg and then the other. I tugged the skirt down past the leather thigh straps and buckles.

When I looked back up, when I was ready, for a second I saw his mouth. It was a perfect Saturday morning cartoon character's circle of impending doom. Then he turned and ran away. I watched as he bumped through the other dancers and disappeared. Each of my friends, at different angles away from me, away from each other, stared into her own distance. I pulled on the spring releases for my knees, sat back down, and joined them.

A quarter of a century later I'm at a classic late-eighties lesbian feminist potluck. Zucchini bread, brown rice with stir-fried vegetables, and pasta with pesto made from the basil crop of one of our gardens are served up on plates we balance on our laps. Our glasses of hibiscus tea sit on the floor beside our chairs. The newsletter committee is looking for somewhere to put on a fundraising dance. Suggestions of various church halls and bars fold into a discussion about the dances of our past. One of us, an ex–high school cheerleader, remembers sexual objectification. How bad it made her feel. How it still affects her relationship with a lover. Around me there are nods of agreement and mutterings of "assholes" and "damaging patriarchal crap."

One woman tells her own story of a mother who pushed her daughter's looks forward as a way of jumping class. I stare into the distance. I think about the damage of growing up without ever having been sexually objectified. How can I explain this?

"Hey," I begin, "objectify me. Talk about my great tits and my perfect nipples and the thoughts they make you think. Say you wish my shorts were just a little bit shorter, so you could catch a glimpse of the good stuff. Moan and hoot when I bend over to pick up this glass of tea. Really, objectify me."

Complex Math

In my senior year of high school I was the plain friend of the cute girl. She had ironed hair bleached margarine-yellow, and behind a poof of bangs, along the center part, was a full inch of dark roots. She wore push-up bras and eye makeup that included black lines drawn down from her lower eyelids. I helped her with those. I had a steady hand. Cute girls keep plain girls close because we're helpful, no competition, and serve as protection. But I look at photos now, and in headshots we weren't that different on the scale of late 1960s, white-girl pretty, and I know my breasts were bigger.

Sometimes boys in cars would come alongside as I drove my parents' green Oldsmobile station wagon. They would smile. They would whistle. I relished these moments of being a normal girl. Once a carload followed me into the Woolworth's parking lot. When I opened the door, flipped out a crutch, and pulled my body to standing in one smooth move, the car screeched away. This sort of thing was still a shock to me, though I'd always felt the schism between who I was and how people saw me. Still, as a kid, I could pretend to ignore all that and still feel graceful and strong like a gymnast as I stretched my arms out to take long, sidewalk-eating strides or balanced over one crutch to carry a school lunch tray without spilling. With adolescence came the new bounce of breasts and the way my pelvis and belly hummed with what I now know was lust. It was as if there were a glow inside me. But in high school it was harder to be unthinking and immersed in the pleasure of movement and sensation.

Once one of the boys got out of his car. For a moment I thought he was going to flirt, maybe ask for my number, but he shuffled over to me and muttered an apology from under a bent head. Noticing me the way a boy notices a girl seemed to be the offense. His ears were red enough to cast a pink shadow against his neck. Now I realize he was a polite boy, well raised by his mother to be respectful, but the ones who screeched tires in their panic to leave were less cruel. I learned more than ever to blur the reflection from other people's eyes—to mute anger, to mute hope.

The cute girl and I lived in a Georgia country town that was transitioning into a bedroom suburb of Atlanta. She had lived in this place all her life, but I was a newcomer. We'd moved there when my father retired from the military. In this school girls were not permitted to wear pants, so my mother bought me a maxicoat to protect my legs on cold days. The assistant principal called her. Maxicoats were on the list, along with culottes and fringed jackets, of banned attire. Every morning the loudspeaker announced a list of transgressive boys whose sideburns were too long. A classmate who got married couldn't return to school without a doctor's certificate stating she wasn't pregnant. It was as if, with regulations ranging from the egregious to the petty, they were trying to hold off the world.

The cute girl liked that I got to use my parents' car. We'd drive the station wagon down to Piedmont Park in Atlanta and score from white hippies. Any of them wearing a dashiki had drugs for sure, we thought (a racist code equating anything black to drug dealing). I stayed back, and she stepped forward. As they moved toward her, I heard giggling and low murmurs. We always got our drugs for free. The cute girl understood her power over these almost men, and she was aware of the danger. When a guy's tone became singsong and rough, she stepped closer to me.

The guys stared at me standing to the side with my elbows leaning on top of my crutches. I stared past them all the way to the tongueless place inside me. I was jealous of their ease with her. I was again outside of what was happening. I didn't understand the tightrope of desire and violence she walked in the dusk, just off the path, in an urban park, but I sensed its pull on her and how this, more than the drugs, was the reason she wanted to be here. As I waited for the transaction to end, I felt a boredom prickled through with anger.

The cute girl and I drove home and spent the night crowded into my single bed. We took the acid, and even as a swirl of colors lifted up out of my own body, I had to be the one to talk her down. I could use only urgent whispers, what with my parents asleep in the next room. It was stressful. The good thing, the thing that made her worthwhile to me, was that sometimes, if she were high enough, we'd kiss.

That year in senior English we had to write a short story. So I wrote about this. Not the kissing, of course, but about two friends who hang around in a park and get drugs. I tried to show how drab it all was. It was odd to pull words out of a wordless place and to be honest about something, anything. It seemed that if I was going to write, this was how it had to be. The days after handing it in, waiting, I was fitful. The world had become even more precarious.

The teacher called me aside after class. He had my paper in his hand. Even before he started talking, horror spread over my skin like sweat. I stared at the way his thumb wrinkled into the thin, lined notebook paper, and then I stared at his face. It was hard to hear him. Like a movie with the sound out of synch, the words made sense seconds after he spoke them. "You have some nice descriptions here. But the whole piece is told in a monotone." His lips went still. Something had made him stop talking. My eyes followed as he lifted the paper close enough to read. His thumb moved off into the margin. He mouthed and then I heard, "Unless, of course, you meant it to be that way." I have no memory of what happened next, but I know I didn't say anything. Perhaps I shrugged. All I wanted was for him to give me the paper back.

I do remember that he reported me to the school counselor. She was mostly the math teacher, so it was at her desk, in her classroom, that she questioned me. She was one of the young and modern teachers and had a kind face. She told me I could talk to her about anything. I looked at her steady on and swore that it was fiction, that I had made the whole thing up from things I'd read in the newspaper. I tried to solve the algebra equations on the blackboard while she decided what to do. Perhaps the very tediousness of my writing made her believe me. She didn't make an official report. I didn't get suspended. I didn't lose my college scholarship. It was thirty-five years before I took another writing course.

Atlanta—1984

Another lesbian and I drive along Ponce de Leon Avenue. We're on our way to an antiapartheid rally downtown. We pass the old Sears building and stop at the light. She points and says, "A long time ago there was a lesbian bar right there. It was a rough place—the type with fights and police raids." I turn to look. Through the window I see the new Super Kroger, but reflected in the glass, my fifteen-year-old face looks back at me. It's pressed against the window, wanting. I think about that woman. Maybe she saw me staring. Maybe she understood. Whoever she was, I thank her for standing queer on the street.

Becoming Lazy

Each evening for years, coming home from my bookstore, I'd bend my elbows, wedge both crutch tips into the concrete, and pull my feet onto the walkway that led to the door of my apartment. It was a small curb that hardly broke my stride, but that day strength fell out of my arms like water. I was left dangling with one more inch to clear. I stiffened my back, and what abdominal power I had pulled at my thighs. Tendons stretched away from their joints as I grunted out a last-ditch lunge. All I achieved was a suspended moment free from the laws of gravity before my heels smacked back down onto the ground. I teetered backward. Just in time, I stabbed one crutch behind me and the other to the side. Both shoulders twisted in their sockets. I hovered at the edge of collapse until my hips pulled back to center. I was safe.

But I didn't know what to do next. If I didn't figure out how to get up that lip of concrete, my life would fall apart. I refused to think about that. I refused to think of how my life was already falling apart. I lowered my head and scouted for another approach. To my left, the turf was higher and decreased the rise by at least an inch. I positioned myself. I lifted my crutches onto the concrete again and leaned forward to test their placement. I moved my feet farther away from the edge to widen the angle of my elbows. How open could they be and still lift my body into the air? Did I need to keep them tucked into my side? I shuffled back to my original position. I'd never had to think this way before.

Once, I read a book on meditation. It told me to control my breathing, to be aware. I had set the book down and sucked in air. I let some out and then more. I waited. Had I inhaled for too long? Had I exhaled enough? Too much? My throat collapsed, and the back of my eyes went dry. Before I figured out to breathe again, I had almost fainted. It was like that now, trying to figure out what had always been automatic.

My muscles stopped quivering. It was time. There was only one more try left in me. At the top of a long breath, I began. The crutch tips gripped the curb. The weight lifted off my legs, and my toes scraped up the edge, but one foot wedged into a place the concrete had crumbled. The other, the stronger one, made it over the top. I used it to twist until both feet were side by side. On the same held breath, I rushed to my door, unlocked it, and then locked it behind me as if I'd escaped an intruder. Relief cascaded through my body as I leaned against a wall. The shaking started in my belly that was always the prelude to crying.

I stiffened my back, pushed off the wall, and did what I'd been doing every day after work for months, a year maybe. Had it been longer? I peed, threw back a handful of anti-inflammatories, and dropped onto the bed. I took off my braces and clothes. I pulled a blanket up to my shoulders and stared at the ceiling while pain and exhaustion and sweat soaked into the bedding. The old fear rose. It had always, as long as I could remember, been with me, but now, in my adult years, I'd contained it within a name: the "nursing home and bedsores" panic. I said it in a mocking tone of voice directed at myself. A swollen knuckle, a fall that jammed up my elbow, a costly broken stirrup on my brace that left my shoe dangling—stop worrying, I would say, what do you think, that tomorrow you'll be in a nursing home with bedsores? It was my personal image of the apocalypse. But that day I hurt more. My body smelled bad. I had almost been unable to get into my own home.

Swimming would make everything better. It always had. The problem was, I decided, that working sixty-hour weeks had left me out of shape, and I needed to exercise. I went to the Y for early morning laps and left my braces in the locker room. Using just my crutches and the one leg that would hold straight at the knee, I slid along the walls to get to the pool. The other lappers watched me stagger. I knew they thought I'd mess up the flow of their lanes, but I swam for longer distances than most of them. I wasn't the fastest, but I wasn't the slowest. Until I was.

Soon it took a day's worth of energy to get to the side of the pool. And then I couldn't get to the side of pool. There were falls at home. That was okay. But one day I was standing in front of the science fiction section at work with one elbow resting on top of my crutch, using my freed-up arm to hand a customer the latest Octavia Butler novel. As we were discussing our mutual interest in her Patternmaster series and how, of course, nothing compared to Kindred, my body tilted. I pushed on my crutches and shifted my hips automatically, but the usual adjustments didn't work except to turn the fall into a slow motion event. I watched the customer's jaw fall, also in slow motion, and then, somehow, I was on the floor. It seemed that I couldn't reliably walk anymore. What did this mean?

What it meant, eventually, was that I wrote a poem. It was about a woman's fingers, how "they wrapped themselves around my brace / Around the stretch of metal where it thins / And curves past my ankle." The fifteen lines of muddy imagery and uninspired line breaks thrilled me. And all it took to accomplish this was for me to move to a new apartment, build a ramp to it, and get a manual wheelchair.

The man who fitted the wheelchair, as he kneeled in front of me to check the length of my thighs, shook his head, tsked, and told me that I should try not to become lazy. I grabbed the wheels and wondered if it would break his nose if I snapped the wheelchair forward. His comment was ignorant and inappropriate. He was an asshole. But mostly I wanted him kicked back on his butt, holding his face and yowling, because I hated that I agreed with him. I relaxed my fists from around the rims and as was my long custom, spoke calmly and made sure he did his job and set me up with the lightweight, sporty chair I wanted.

At first, I kept the wheelchair in the back of my car and pulled it out only to go grocery shopping. The cashiers, the deli staff, the other shoppers—they were always smiling at me. Was this some new thing I was learning, that people in wheelchairs got smiled at all the time? The public had often smiled at me when I used crutches, but those were too-wide smiles that looked as if invisible hooks were pulling at the corners. The men who kneeled, grabbed one of my crutches, held on, and prayed to "the Lord" for my healing while I struggled to get away had these types of smiles. And these grocery store smiles weren't the grimaced ones of people averting their eyes, embarrassed to be caught staring.

My brain searched for an analysis of people's attitude about disability that would explain this crutch/wheelchair smile difference. One day, reaching for raspberry yogurt, I nodded at the woman beside me. I was smiling at her. Perhaps that was the difference. If you were in less pain, you smiled more. And when you smiled at people, they smiled back. Smiling might be just the beginning. If I used the wheelchair more, if I was in less pain, maybe I would be smart again, maybe I could think past making it through the next few hours, maybe I would dream again of a future—a future I couldn't yet imagine. It was 1987. I was thirty-five.

Rolling in the Mud

I've never touched the earth much. Water, yes. As a child I'd unbuckle kneepads and thigh straps to lift my legs out of their braces. My skin hissed as it pulled away from the brushed leather of thigh cuffs. With braces and crutches left in a jumble off to the side, I'd crawl into snow-fed lakes with sudden, immense depths. The abeyance of gravity smoothed the indentations left by aluminum rods designed to untwist and make plumb, and my legs spread into their own natural akimbo shape. These days I slip out of a wheelchair and into Florida waters. Spring-fed rivers warm or cool, depending on the season, and Atlantic waves toss me until the seafloor scrapes against my skin and saltwater burns my lungs. Summertimes in the bathtub-warm and gentle Gulf, I lie on my back, glasses off, stare at the now hazy, impressionist sky, and float with no effort the way fat women can.

But it's not often that I touch the earth directly. Sometimes my hands dig at the surface to plant or pull in my yard. More often the contact is less immediate: still connected, but once removed. A friend digs for me, her shovel hits a root, and I hear the thud of metal and see the sudden strain in her forearms. Driving over the washboard ripple of a dirt road after rain can shake the topography of a landscape into my bones. Or my kayak will nose into the high-tide openings of salt marshes until maiden cane tangles the paddle and black needlerush leans in to itch over my knuckles. Sometimes I search out the narrow reaches of black-water creeks, where leather fern spores bronze my shoulders. And now and again, the rasp of littoral grasses at the edge of a lake sounds into the keel of my boat and feathers the backside of my thighs.

The La Chua Trail into Paynes Prairie is one of my places of least remove from the earth. Here I first saw a bald eagle, a lotus in bloom, a whooping crane. I've pushed my wheelchair past two hundred alligators lined along the trail, their heads following me in slow motion, while friends and I make jokes about looking as little like poodles as possible. That year when low water levels attracted hundreds of wood storks, I went day after day to see the fluffed necks of the young ones, and it's not unusual for a water moccasin to raise a warning head out of the grass alongside one of my wheels. In 1989 I moved to Florida. The Prairie is one of the reasons why.

I first traveled the trail in a manual chair, then in a scooter, and now in a power wheelchair. When I hear the hiss of sand under my wheels, feel the sink and pull, I know to shift my weight and turn onto a clump of grass that congeals the surface and gives traction. I traveled this trail before there were signs or gates. I traveled it before the state built an observation deck with steps instead of a ramp. It blocks the piece of dry ground where I used to perch each winter to look over the marsh and watch thousands of sandhill cranes mix with occasional groups of white pelicans. And now a vista-destroying boardwalk snakes around Alachua Sink, but it is still a place of connection. I still travel here.

All the seasons on Paynes Prairie have touched me. The purple and yellow days are in the spring—swaths of marsh marigold and spikes of pickerelweed. You have to go in the summer to see the lotus. The June weight of air in my lungs is a comfort even as sweat slicks the vinyl of the armrests and stings along my spine. September, still summer in Florida, is always a judgment call.

Clouds, black and shot through with a metallic green, tower into the sky, and I brace against downdraft winds to watch the last sunlight at the edge of a storm. It races across the Prairie tinting the oranges from rust to tangerine, the yellows to neon. It's only when lightning strikes close that I can turn away. Full speed, leaning forward over the controls as if that will make the chair go faster, heedless of hips and back, I bounce over the trail to my van. If I've timed it right, I'm closing the doors before the first, fat raindrops turn into a voice-drowning rush against the metal roof. Once, in the season of government-controlled burns, a sheer curtain line of fire came close, so thin that it seemed possible to leap through it. The inner structure of the air changed as ions shifted. It crackled the hairs along my arms. It was as if I were on another planet. Sometimes in the winter there are cold days that make my bones ache. Alligators burrow in the mud to stay warm, the low humidity blues the sky, and egret and ibis white glints against the eyes.

In the late nineties, the Prairie flooded. It wasn't like in 1873. Then the Alachua Sink that drains the Prairie blocked and stayed that way for almost twenty years until, in a sudden drop, the lake disappeared and left steamboats, waterfront tourist attractions, and thousands of fish stranded. For us, it flooded high and for long enough that water lapped over the outside lanes of the highway that cuts the Prairie in two, and alligators, desperate for any high ground, lay nose up to the traffic. There were daily reports. Would the road crumble apart? Float away? Crack? I wanted it to. I wanted to witness the Prairie become once again the Great Alachua Savanna. This did not happen.

But I started searching the road for a place to pull over, yank my kayak out from the back of the van and slip into the water. I imagined leaving my empty wheelchair beside the road as a puzzle for the police or State Park Rangers. All I had to do was get beyond bullhorn range. It would be worth the ticket just to see what it was they charged me with. But I'm not quick, and my van is not stealthy, so I never tried. Of course, I wasn't the only one thinking this way, and eventually the State Park allowed guided trips. I signed up.

When the day comes, I'm early, so it's just Lars and me at the edge of the flood. The water is disorienting. The big oak where I usually park my van and start my strolls is at the new shoreline. Lars, the man who literally wrote the book on the Prairie, is unloading all the rental kayaks while I snap and click the gear into place on my own boat. He has to go unlock the gate for the rest of the people. Will I be okay? Yes, I say. And this is part of why I admire Lars—he believes me. He lets me be on my own. This type of respect is usually something I have to fight for, even threaten lawsuits over. Sometimes in groups Lars introduces me as an outdoorswoman. Of all the things I've ever been called, it is my favorite.

He leaves. I'm alone on the Prairie. It's still rising, they say. There is no one else here. I stare at the water and think I see it creep along the trail. The gate is locked until Lars unlocks it and lets the rest of today's tour in. I don't have long to be alone, but I do have this time. I won't wait. I drop out of my wheelchair and land on the very last of dry earth, at least for today. I scoot on my bottom, pull the kayak, scoot more, pull the kayak. Through my nylon pants, under my bare hands, the ground becomes first cooler, then wet.

This isn't a regular lake edge. No pennywort laps through stalks of arrowhead and bull rush anchored in muck. No buttressed trunks of cypress trees line the shore. This has been high ground for a hundred years. The spiderworts, star and pepper grasses, accustomed to sun-baked sand, are dying under the water, but their roots hold firm in earth that is reluctant to become mud. Again my arms lift the weight of my body, and this time my palms press through sand into water. The path is becoming lake bottom. I pull the bow to me and lean against it as a red-tailed hawk screams past. This used to be a dry meadow that provided mice and snakes. It will be again. This lake won't exist forever. These events, which have led to me being alone, here, on the ground, are as ephemeral. I listen for engines, but it's too soon to expect anyone.

I lie on my back, knees bent. A thin skin of water ripples down it. My legs flop to the side, my hip follows, and now my breasts are against the earth. My body mixes the wilted grasses with the soil. I roll again, and my shoulder blades sink into the smoothness of dissolving plantain leaves. I spread my arms, and rotting grasses wrap around them. A twist of my head and I'm at eye-level with everything I used to wheel over. Another roll farther into the water and wet slides along my ribs and covers my wrists. And now I think about an alligator swimming and searching for dry land.

I reverse direction until my elbows scrape into hard sand and the stiff edges of hedge-nettle and Spanish needle. I lift onto my elbows and look around. I can see for a long ways. There are no alligators. I leave the myth of safety on high ground and roll back into the new mud. I stretch out flat, face up. Am I an agent of erosion? Am I joining water and land? My arms reach over my head until my fingertips brush into the loosened fibers of earth, and muscles pull in a stretch that I usually feel only in bed. It tugs at my flanks and below my belly where my thighs and hips are in an unaccustomed straight line. The underside of both knees aches, a good ache, with extension. My head falls and creates a well of water that laps at my earlobes.

Lars's old van rattles over the gravel. I squirm to sitting, readjust my clothes, pull strands of brown grass off my shoulders and push the kayak through wilting dog fennel to a floatable depth. I splash the less muddy water over my front to clean up a bit. Leaning on the kayak, I kneel over it and tumble and twist into the seat. My knees are the last part of me pressed into the watery earth of Paynes Prairie.

For hours we paddle through fields of lotus and alongside the sunken steps of the observation tower. Attached to the drowning branches of elderberry, gelatinous balls of frog eggs rock in the slow wake of our boats. I stop paddling. The others are ahead of me. I lean toward the bow to ease my back, and my face lowers over my knees and into the oily plant stains and heavy velvet smell of the shoreline. The kayak, responding to the shifts of my body, the wind, the pull of imperceptible currents, turns itself around. Behind us, where we've just traveled, alligators rise.

I'm home. It's evening. I've hosed the sand and slime off the boat, rinsed the paddle, and untangled rotting morning glory from around the bowline. My body is showered and smells only of oatmeal soap and chlorinated water. I'm going to sprinkle baking soda over the laundry, but I hold the clothes against my nose one last time. The water will rise over where I was today and then fall away. What will the path look like when it emerges? Will there have been time for sagittaria to root and grow tall over the water? Will the purple, white, and yellow of bladderworts skim the surface to either side? As I roll over a barely dry trail, shifting away from the patches of mud that remain, will my front wheels dip and lift out of the lingering physical memory of my body? Perhaps lotus will have spread close to the path. I'll perch at the edge of my seat, anchor one arm around the backrest, and lean over the water that remains to reach the oval petals and touch into the swirl of orange-stalked stamens at their center. I close the washing machine lid and set the rinse water to hot.

Open-Water Swimmers

The more I used the wheelchair, the more my life expanded. I had clean clothes. I could grocery shop again. By late 1987 I'd retired my braces and crutches to a back corner of the closet and settled myself into using the manual wheelchair on an exclusive basis. Bathrooms were no longer to be taken for granted, so I learned to dehydrate myself before going out. Friends couldn't have me over anymore. One of my customers cried when she first saw me using the wheelchair. No one knew how to hug me. The day came when I used my wheelchair in my family's presence for the first time. We sat around the kitchen table, and no one spoke to me. Among all the too-quick chatter, I was invisible. But then the four-year-old nephew asked, "Where are your sticks, Auntie?" In simple words, as the adults listened, I said it worked better for me this way, that I could get around places again, that I didn't fall anymore. Then no one talked at all. There was only the wet snap and grind of teeth chewing until my mother asked who wanted ice cream.

Meanwhile, I spun around the aisles of my bookstore with stacks of new arrivals on my lap loaded high enough to pin in place with my chin. Unpacking this many books used to take me four trips. With the right momentum and the perfect grab onto the edge of the new arrivals bookshelf, my wheelchair swept along the wall of women's fiction without me having to touch the wheels. I'd glide to a stop in front of Virginia Woolf and laugh with the joy of easy movement. I felt like an ice skater. I could work long hours again. I started wearing dresses in a way I hadn't since I was forced to in high school. Breezes wrapped themselves around my bared, braceless calves and traveled under my skirts. I wrote an essay about intimacy and then more poems. At the height of this particular arc of possibility, I traveled by myself. Despite the hesitancy of the world around me, I negotiated my way into adventures.

At the edge of the Okefenokee Swamp a park ranger rents canoes, rings up sales, answers phones and people's questions, and is already eyeing me and my wheelchair in that here's-a-prospective-hassle way. I wait in the canoe rental line and hope, but doubt, that the woman will offer to help launch a boat. She's young, and my chances are better with women over fifty and all men. As I reach the head of the line, another ranger, an older man, lets himself behind the counter and takes the woman's place. He brushes a crumb off the front of his uniform and looks over my head to smile at the customer behind me.

"I'd like a four-hour rental." I speak distinctly but refuse to raise my voice. The ranger adjusts the direction of his greeting downward. First advantage goes to me.

"Fiberglass or aluminum?"

"Aluminum." I'm decisive despite having no opinion. He hands over the paperwork, and I pull it down to my lap. The man fidgets with his forms and clears his throat. I keep my head bent.

"How many will be in the canoe?"

"Oh, it's just me." Through my eyelashes, I can see the man's knuckles rub back and forth on the counter.

"Have you canoed before?"

After a pause, I lift my head enough to catch his eye, raise one eyebrow, and say nothing.

He continues, now with a hint of stammering. "I mean, here in the Okefenokee Swamp."

The other ranger pauses in her work. The crowd behind us is listening. As usual, I want to ask if he questions the competence of all adult renters, but he has the power to refuse me service. Sure, I could write a letter of complaint, report him, make an outraged phone call, but I'd be sitting at home doing it. I don't want to fight. I want to go canoeing. I'll throw him a bone.

"Oh, sure. I did that Kingfisher–Bluff Lake overnighter. The pitcher plants were blooming. Amazing, aren't they? Especially the trumpets, I'd never seen them that tall."

I'm not lying, although I would. An ex-lover had arranged for the camping trip. The best part of our relationship had been her enthusiasm for all things outdoors. She'd known the Latin names of everything and was a fanatic for carnivorous plants. I toss out pieces of my ex's knowledge as a barrier between me and the ranger's prejudices: *Saracenia flava* versus *purpurea*, the underappreciation of sundews, are bladderworts still in flower? Handing over the required ten dollars and completed form, I stop talking. If they take the money, it means something. The ranger spends too much time smoothing the bills, but both he and I sigh as he tucks them into the register.

"If you meet me down there," the man points through the window, "I'll put the canoe in the water. You want to wear a jacket life preserver, right?"

"No, a cushion will do." We smile at each other, and I think "nice try, mister." I'm liking this guy.

We meet at the ramp, and I bark out a laugh as, with a one-sided grin, he throws both a jacket and cushion preserver into the canoe. He holds the side steady, and I swing onto the seat. I fold my chair, and he lifts it into the well of the boat. He waits while I tie it down and then, when I give him a nod, pushes the canoe backward until it floats.

With a wide front sweep of the paddle, I turn the bow into the swamp.

But it doesn't last.

Soon pushing the wheelchair up the hill from the parking lot to the bookstore teetered at the edge of what was physically possible. The creative life scurried away, and the glimpse I'd had of it felt like a cruel joke. Each day how to grocery shop and cook was something to solve. I had staff at the bookstore, but if I used their time to fetch me lunch, was that cheating the store? Was that treating them as servants? I couldn't figure it out. Most days I managed not to cry in public. I trimmed my life to work, getting home, and going back to work, but still my breath was caught up in one long gasp against pain.

Open-water swimmers endure eight-foot waves and fifteen-knot headwinds. They swim for eleven, thirty, fifty-five hours and vomit seawater and cry for their mothers. Jellyfish stings lance over their skin and cramp their muscles. Their minds strip down to hallucinations and the base instinct of taking one stroke after another. Their strokes stay strong even when they don't make any headway. Some, the women especially, develop bodies that survive Antarctic waters by keeping their blood close to the core.

Pass the Hemlock

I leaned over to Eleanor and whispered, "Check out that guy's hardware." We both looked at the man's tricked-out wheelchair with its fancy electronics. Eleanor chucked her chin at a woman who sat on the edge of her wheelchair, poised, breasts out, knees tilted together and to the side. "And check out that one's software." We laughed behind our hands since we were probably the only lesbians at the postpolio support group meeting.

But then the presenter came in. She was one of those old, no-crap-allowed doctors. She didn't waste our time.

"Don't do anything that leaves you with pain or muscle fatigue or a sense of weakness that lasts more than ten minutes. That's the rule. Otherwise you're just digging yourselves into a hole."

All of us stared at her. There were clipped laughs from behind me. She stared right back at us.

"Listen, all of you have exhaustive exercise damage, just like any other high-end athlete. Only you get it doing your activities of daily living. But chemically and neurologically, it's the same. The methods of recovery are well documented, as are the sequelae of ignoring them."

The audience turned surly.

"You sure don't have teenagers at home."

"You're talking about never leaving my bed for who knows how long."

"My physical therapist says I'm getting lazy, that I should be doing more."

"I'd have to quit my job. Are you going to pay my bills?"

The physician's voice reached over the outrage. "It's not all bad news. You can regain some strength. But only if you stop the damage. Every time you overdo, there is inflammation and muscle fiber degeneration. That's where the no pain, no fatigue comes in. And even then regeneration will begin only one to two weeks after you reach that baseline. This is how muscles work. There are no short cuts or ways to avoid it. And that physical therapist you in the corner mentioned, fire her."

That time the room stayed silent until a wry voice came from the back.

"Well, pass me the hemlock now."

The whole room laughed, and the doctor's face gentled for the first time.

"I started my career working the polio epidemics. All of you kids, you were scared a lot. We made mistakes in how we handled that. It's likely that you're going to relive some of the fear as your body changes again. But this woman, what she just said, is evidence of what has always been true. You people have highly developed skills at adapting, including a sense of humor. You can adapt again."

As I left the meeting, I heard a man mutter to his wife, "That was interesting, but the lady doctor didn't mean no pain at all. That's impossible."

His wife's face defined the look "long suffering." Inside myself, I was both husband and wife as I rushed back to work.

The coils of phone cord snaked under my armpit. I trapped them in place with an elbow tight against my side, which left enough slack for the receiver to stay tucked under my chin. My mother was on the other end. I made "uh, huh" noises into the receiver while I watched over the customers. It was the Christmas rush of 1987, and even a feminist bookstore was eager for the boost of profligate spending. The shoppers were like cats on catnip with their aimless wanderings down the aisles interrupted by sudden strikes. Somehow, by mistake, my partners and I had set up a schedule where I was alone. But one of them, my recent ex, was expected later.

"And I even trimmed back the forsythia bush yesterday since it was sunny. Then I polished the brass. One has to keep busy since things can feel a little low on the weekends when you're a widow. Widow, that's an odd word, isn't it?"

"Uh, huh." A woman placed her list in front of me and tapped her pen on the line that said "ten-year-old boy." I hunched my shoulder against my neck as tight as I could, wheeled to the far side of the cash register and stretched the phone cord until I could grab a copy of *Juggling for the Complete Klutz* off a shelf. I handed it to her. When I lifted my hands off the wheels, the cord snapped the chair back toward the counter. I bumped into a spinner rack.

"But tomorrow is Bingo, and Wednesday is the class on First Ladies. We're all the way to Lady Bird. I always sit next to the same woman, it's nice to have a friend, and last week she had such good news. Her son is moving in with her since her eyesight is getting bad, and he's going to drive her around and shop, and he's even a cook. Isn't she lucky to have children that will take care of her? You had to work this weekend, I presume."

"No, I had both days off, for once. I really needed it."

"Both days." My mother's voice went flat.

That I had made a bad tactical error and that it was too late to lie became simultaneously obvious. The customer with the list came back with a pile of merchandise and tipped it all onto the counter. She tapped her pen on the glass.

"Mother, I have to go help this customer."

"Wait. What time will you be here Christmas Eve? I've put fresh sheets on the bed for you. That back corner is such a bother, but I managed it. How about six?"

"Uh, huh. No, wait. Mother, we talked about this. I work that day. It's better I rest, and I promise, I'll leave very first thing in the morning."

"I don't understand the difference, dear. It's the same drive whenever you make it."

I covered the receiver and mouthed "my mother" at the customer. She left the counter. I was being a terrible clerk. If I were my own employee, I would have fired myself. I uncovered the mouthpiece.

"Remember, Mother, those articles I gave you about post-polio. What they said about pacing oneself?" My voice, to my annoyance, had become wavery and high-pitched.

"Is that still going on?"

"What do you mean?"

"Are you still tired? This seems to be going on forever. All I ever hear from you is how tired you are."

The customer returned, plopped a box of Georgia O'Keeffe note cards on top of her pile and waited.

"I have to go, Mother." I tried not to sound like I was begging.

"Well, so do I. I'm making beef stew, and it's time to put in the barley. I made enough for us to have for Christmas Eve dinner, but I guess I'll put it in the freezer. It's never as good that way."

The phone went dead. I started in on my apologies to the waiting customer, but she put her hand down on the counter close to mine.

"Tidings of good joy?"

She said it in such a kind voice that I almost cried. I blinked a few times and then put myself back into retail mode.

"Okay, what's next on that list of yours?"

For six hours I worked the store. I sold coming-out books to a college lesbian going home to her family for the holidays, a tarot deck to a single father whose daughter was visiting for the holiday, and the entire collection of Nicole Hollander cartoon books to a woman who decided her mother needed them. I answered phone calls about hours, special orders, and gay bars. I thwarted a shoplifter and used my vigorous dusting of the shelves technique to evict a creepy guy from the women's sexuality section. As each customer approached the counter, I smiled and cast around for a way to up the sale amount. I profiled people shamelessly by how they looked and what they were buying. A white woman in a teal silk shirt tied with a bow handed over a credit card. It was in her husband's name. This woman had discretionary income.

"Oh, you like Marge Piercy! Have you read her latest novel? How about her poetry?" We went back to the shelves together and tripled her original purchase. I was the queen of my realm.

A regular came in and wanted four gifts under ten dollars, and when I asked her who they were for, she said it didn't matter, just something general, and quick. She had to be walking out of the store within five minutes. I grabbed my wheels, pirouetted, and before coming out of the spin, had gathered a Sierra Club calendar, a box of greeting cards with oil paintings of fruit, a journal with a silk embroidered cover, and a paperback copy of *Mists of Avalon*. The customer was already filling in her check. I tried to show her the selections, but she waved me off.

"Just bag them and give me the total."

It was December, the annual fleecing of the Christians. Seeing this customer, who usually took time to sit with her selections and read through them and often wanted to discuss, at length, the latest May Sarton journal, giving gifts this way—with no caring or connection—and using a tone with me that was almost rude, this was the sort of thing that made me sure I was immorally benefiting from rampant, guilt-induced consumerism, that I was nothing but a cog contributing to the overall decline of society. But each evening, I'd close out the register and lose myself in the capitalist slut thrill of counting large stacks of money. Some bills were crisp and hard to separate from each other. Some had "lesbian money" scrawled over the serial number. Most were soft and worn through at the fold. And the money wasn't just money. A mixture of perfumes, human sweat, and wallet leather lifted into the air as I turned the presidents' heads in the same direction and tapped the stacks even. It was an anonymous, yet intimate, connection to people.

The woman ripped out her check and snatched the bag off the counter. The phone rang again. It was my sister.

"You need to stop saying that you're tired. It upsets Mother. She thinks you'll have to move back in with her, and she'll end up taking care of you for the rest of her life."

I smashed the disconnect button and threw the receiver down. It bounced. My ex had just come in the door. There was only so much I could handle at once, although so far we'd maintained a polite manner with each other in the store. When the relationship before this one was ending, I'd stopped drinking, and this was helping with the emotional murkiness of having to work with an ex. I took a breath and modulated my voice.

"It's been crazy busy today."

"Well, I can't help yet. I came in early to do my own work."
She walked past the counter and headed to the office.

"Hey." My tone was sharp enough to stop her. "I wasn't asking for help. I was just sharing good news."

"Oh, sorry. Still, pretend I'm not here."

"No problem with that." I muttered this to an already-closed office door.

For once, there were no customers at the counter. I let my head fall forward into a long stretch that pulled between my shoulder blades.

"The phone needs hanging up."

My ex's voice came from the back. No "please." No "when you get a chance." I kept my head down but turned it toward her. She'd cracked the office door and, from my sideways view, I could see a four-inch strip of cheek, shoulder, knee, and chair leg. Sometimes it was hard to remember that we'd ever been lovers. I looked around and found the phone dangling off the side of my wheelchair. I slid a section of cord out from under one of the push handles and lifted an armrest to untangle another length. I took my time, a lot of time. I pulled until it uncoiled from around a brake lever, but it stayed stuck under a front caster. I rolled back until it released. I gathered the loops into one arm and held them high, away from the spokes, and leaned over to dump the tangle onto the shelf. I patted escaping coils back into place for longer than needed. And then I put the receiver on the base.

"It's all yours." The "asshole" I tagged on was quiet enough that even the closest customer only thought she heard it.

A door can't be slammed properly with just a four-inch start, but she tried. It was most likely because of the accounts payable. She'd probably seen where I ordered way too many calendars.

Or that I dumped a returns order in her inbox. She'd put both on her list of complaints for the next staff meeting. These days it made each of us happy to find a mistake the other had made. I used to be the one who hardly ever made any, but I'd become careless and forgot so much. Who knew what she was uncovering? I decided to go back there and check. Perhaps I had a defense for whatever I'd done. Maybe I could bring myself to apologize if I had to.

I put my hand up to open the office door. She was still on the phone. She whispered, but I heard my name. It made me feel defeated. I went back to the front and waited on more customers.

The neighbor's security light comes through the frosted bathroom window and lies in a glow alongside the bed. My bladder aches. Is it late evening? Early morning? Either way, I have to move. Within the bluish shadows, I see my hand rise and then flop onto my belly. I feel my belly, but not the hand. Okay. It's okay. Your arms have gone numb, that's all. Be patient. I rotate my shoulders and flex the muscles in my arms until my hands can wave above me in a blunt, undirected way. I lift onto one elbow, but it collapses underneath me, and I drop back, hips twisted, my arm pinned between my ribs and the mattress. I fight at the smothering in my chest.

"Just claustrophobia. Ride it out. Work the arms harder. There's no problem here." The squeezed shrill of my speaking voice frightens me.

A shiver rides down my body and shakes under my skin until a translucent outline rises out of my torso and sits above me with its lower half still submerged into my pelvis. My shadow image rocks over me. The rocking becomes violent. The shadow flails over my hips. I hear screaming. I look through the shadow and into the reds of the Georgia O'Keeffe poster on the far wall. Am I dreaming? Can anyone else hear the screaming? The frenzy diminishes, the movements slow, and with a final high-pitched keen over my body, the shadow sinks back into me. When I can move, I go to the bathroom. It's four in the morning. I turn on the overhead and bedside lights and get dressed for work.

On the disability application the pages and pages of forms asked circular questions. What were my hobbies? Did I work? Did I do my own housekeeping? What were my daily routines? What meals did I prepare? They were designed to catch me in a lie. What did the government think, that someone would slip up and admit to marathon running or square-dance competitions? I must have adequately depicted my life as one of not being able to do anything ever, because the notice came for the doctor's inspection.

The letter ordered me to bathe and wear clean clothes. I warded off humiliation by deconstructing the logic of the letter. Most people would come to the doctor's office fairly clean. If we couldn't get in a shower or get our laundry done or if it was hard to change our clothes, how was this order going to affect that? Wasn't that, perhaps, a reason we were applying? And if we hated doctors and how they'd treated us, and showing up dirty was a way of evening the score, the letter was only going to make us add on another layer of grime.

The doctor told me to hold my arm in the air while he pushed down. I stabilized my torso by gripping the edge of the exam table with my other hand. The doctor noticed me doing this and pushed my arm away. In his I'm-a-doctor-and-just-so-busy voice he said that now he was going to have to start over. He said he'd never had anyone trying to fake being better than they were. I said I wasn't faking. I reminded him that he'd asked me to hold my arm in the air. He hadn't said how, and this was how I did that. All my years of presenting as strong, capable, and not really disabled at all had left me unprepared for this test. But I passed. Or perhaps the correct word is failed. I qualified for Social Security Disability Insurance. I was removed from the workforce.

Poster Children

We're in single file, led by an American flag with stars in the shape of a wheelchair, and headed to the convention hotel that I still think we're going to picket. I joke that this is my first demonstration with a flag waving rather than being worn as pants. Only a few people laugh. The pace increases, and I slip farther back in the line. I can't keep up. Kate's husband comes up behind me and pushes. Eleanor is now far ahead of me, still at the head of the line. I'm jealous of her scooter.

We arrive. Long dining tables are turned on their sides to block the driveway. Police cars are parked behind them. I wonder where we'll form the picket line. Everyone speeds up. Kate's husband is jogging. He slips me through a gap in the barricades and rushes me up the driveway. A police van screeches to an angled stop in front of us. And now all I can think about is how to get past it. I ask Willie to jump me up the curb to the sidewalk. "I'm going on," I say. Willie drops back. I whip around, and my footrests bump into a waiting police officer. "Excuse me," I say automatically. I move to the left. He does as well.

A guy in one of those sports chairs with dramatically cambered wheels screams at me to get out of the way. I don't know how he plans on getting by, but I retreat. The guy knows his stuff because he uses his speed to execute two sharp turns and is past the van and officer. He races for the hotel's front doors. A bunch of us have made it through. I see Eleanor almost there.

Her scooter must be in its power surge setting because her hair is blown back by the speed. My cop goes after them. He leaves the way open, and I know I have to follow Eleanor. I grip my wheels and lunge forward. I feel the wind in my hair.

2.

Eleanor had called to say the ADAPT action was happening, and I should drive the two hours to join them. ADAPT is a group of disability rights activists who think people are better off living in their own homes. Eleanor said the plan was to picket a nursing home convention and disrupt a bunch of CEOS using their monopoly on Medicare funding to guzzle poolside, parasoled drinks. She gave me the name of the hotel where the activists were staying.

I arrived in Orlando and drove down a boulevard lined with miles of Disney World hotels. This is a place that exists only for tourists. There wasn't a grocery, auto shop, or drugstore anywhere. Nothing was in need of paint. It's the early nineties, so everyone I saw was white, and everyone had on shorts with matching tops in solid, primary colors. I pulled into a wide sweep of a driveway where smartly uniformed men greeted me. Even they were white. I waved them off and parked around the corner.

Two of the uniformed men held the doors open and smiled as I pushed my wheelchair through the entrance and glided into the lobby. It glittered with chandeliers as if to greet movie stars. Under their glow were two hundred people in wheelchairs. Almost none of them had on clothes in primary colors except for the red "Free Our People" T-shirts scattered through the crowd. Electric models with space-age controls dashed past hospital clunkers. Some were manuals exactly like mine. A stretcher went by. The person, a woman I think, was wrapped in blankets. Her head, with a bit of wrinkled face showing, was raised just enough to see where she was going as an arthritic hand reached out and pushed a control. There were electric scooters of all sorts. I was attracted to them. They went fast with the push of a finger. I wanted that. People moved themselves all sorts of ways. Palms leaned on a pad, mouths moved a stick, gloved hands gripped wheels, fingers clutched a bar, elbows shoved against a plate, or maybe someone else was pushing their wheelchair, but they were all moving. They were all moving, and they were all shapes and colors and ages.

A grizzled, sullen, toothless old man with what hair he had left pulled back into a gray string of ponytail drooled without shame down the front of his own red T-shirt. It soaked into the image of broken handcuffs. Eleanor slid up beside me. As she leaned over, the handcuffs on her shirt rippled over her chest. She whispered in my ear. "We sprung him from a nursing home and into home care just before they killed him," she said. "He's our poster child." We laughed. She and I had both had polio young and were once the adorable-girl-type of poster child ourselves.

I was introduced to Kate, who held her head pulled down and to the side so what I saw was the top of her close-cropped afro, her eyelashes, and the curve of her nose. She spoke crisp, articulate words in a slurred voice. Her husband and teenage son stood to either side of her. Middle-aged white guys in sports chairs careened around the crowd passing out orders. Eleanor pointed out Lillibet. Her dress was splashed with bright blue and yellow flowers, and she carried a megaphone on her lap. Later she gets arrested for being too loud. Even later I find out she's an antiabortion activist. But right then, we smiled at each other. I had on a blue ball cap that said DYKE across the front in block letters. Lillibet raised her hand, and a Spanish-accented, bull-horned shout told us to line up.

3.

Our cell is bright. Fluorescent tubes hang from the ceiling. They and the cameras stay on all night. The bunks are a freshly painted yellow. The vinyl mattresses are green, and the toilet in the corner is a silvered chrome. The blankets are shades of gray. So are the sheets. We are all in blue, the guards in beige, and the nurse in white. Jennifer's wheelchair is Day-Glo pink.

Renee is telling her jailers how to touch her, how to put her in bed. Her body is small. Her sternum is large and bowed. She has movie-star eyes, and her arms make delicate gestures. I'm watching from the next bunk. I remember her from earlier in the day. She had sat straight in her power chair and led with her chest, while her sister ran behind her and tried to keep up. Her sister is here. The police department's strategy had been to arrest every able-bodied-looking person they could. They figured these people could act as attendants in jail. It was ADAPT's policy that they should refuse. Renee's sister leans against the cell wall. She clasps her hands behind her back. Renee instructs the guards who are standing over her with their arms crossed over their waists and their expressions stern.

"Don't lift me by my arms. Reach around my middle and then under my rear end." Her fingers point around her body to emphasize the instructions.

The guards shift this way and that to search for a less awkward angle. Their legs set in place, and Renee disappears into their arms as they reach over her wheelchair with great care and lift.

They step to the bed and lay her down. From behind them, I hear Renee.

"On my side," she says. "I need pillows to brace my legs."

"No pillows in jail," one of the guards states and then folds a blanket and holds it up.

"That will work." Renee's voice reaches out of the sheets. "Put that one between my legs, and get another for behind my knees."

The rest of her instructions are quiet and practiced. Then the guards bend lower over her bed.

"I'll need to be repositioned later."

The guards cover her with a blanket and turn toward me to leave. From my own bunk, I watch them as they pass by. Both of their faces, one brown and one white, are wide open with emotion. It's not pity or disgust or resentment—I can recognize those. This is less familiar.

The Art of Budgeting

In the nineties I learned to be as disciplined about rest as I had been about work until my life became more than just survival. But I missed how I used to lift my whole body from kneeling with my arms, and I missed going somewhere on a whim without calculating the energy costs and what I'd have to give up later. I had so very little money. I moved out of the city to a small town in Florida where everything was less expensive, where I had friends, and where ospreys nested on telephone poles beside strip malls and the occasional bald eagle marauded its food. New acquaintances asked, as is polite, "And what do you do?" I didn't know how to answer. I mumbled that I was retired. They'd say, "I wish I could retire" with an extended emphasis on the second *I*. I'd think, "Fuck you." These were awkward exchanges.

It was the first time since I was ten and started babysitting that I didn't have a job. But I had a sustainable life again, which meant that I could pay the rent, shop for groceries, cook, and get myself to the library. I didn't have much discretionary income, but this new life offered discretionary energy. Still.

I used to know everything—when the new Toni Morrison would be in paper, who Amanda Cross really was, where a homeless person could get a meal, and the exact chronological order of the Darkover Series. I ordered a million dollars' worth of books, and people bought them. We created a place where it was safe for a woman to rest her chin on a lover's shoulder as they browsed a magazine together, flipping the pages, pointing and murmuring to each other. *Getting Free, Incest and Sexuality, I Never Told Anyone*: these were books customers had brought to the counter. Some slapped them down on the glass, and others held them hidden under an armpit, but either way they told me, entrusted me.

Now I stretched carefully every morning, and hurt flickered along tender joints. Most afternoons I napped. Outside my door slow breezes rattled a palm and moved a spider's web in and out of the sunlight. I fed myself three meals a day as if I were my own child. I missed the weight of the store keys hanging from my belt as if I were the lady of a manor. I missed pride. I missed power.

My mother, in her widowhood, noticed me. She came to visit. She stayed in my Section 8 Housing–funded apartment and managed not to comment. I took her to Marjorie Kinnan Rawlings's home. There wasn't a ramp, so I wandered the grounds while she toured the house. Friends came over for a big potluck and celebrated her. We went to see alligators and flocks of ibis up close. She had a great time. And when I needed it, when the Section 8 regulations became more onerous, she gave me the down payment on a house. I had my own home. I had my own washer and dryer for the first time in my life.

Houses are expensive. Money was harder. But I budgeted aggressively. Meat and air-conditioning I could mostly do without, but I had a high personal standard of gift giving. I found a book in the library on hand-binding journals and taught myself how to make an actual book. It had a hard cover and end papers and an attached ribbon for a bookmark. It seemed a wondrous thing to do. I liked all the new words. The stitches: kettle, Coptic, blanket, and buttonhole. The bindings: laced, stabbed, accordion, and French door.

It was a relief to now, again, have lovely gifts for friends. Some people wanted to buy the journals and that funded a worktable and a cutting mat and a leather thimble for the stab bindings. A bone folder helped make my creases sharp and unwrinkled. I was proud of my deckle edges. Just touching the supplies made any day a good day. I imagined a stranger who received one as a gift. She hadn't known me as a bookstore manager or a person who wore leg braces or now as someone who couldn't work a job. She didn't even know that I used a wheelchair—I was simply the person who had made the journal she held in her hands. Perhaps I had used a coral pink satin cord to make a leaf-patterned Japanese stab binding. I had scored the book boards perfectly and chosen cover papers thick with a burgundy, velvety brocade. Her fingers rubbed over them.

I learned to make my own paper. I ripped up junk mail, mixed it with saved dryer lint, and slurred them together in a blender. Suspend it all in a dishpan of water, dip a screen, and out come sheets of paper. I pressed in dried flowers, grasses, and fronds gathered from neighbors' yard clippings. These became the covers of my journals, rough and wild. Sometimes an insect would hatch out from under a dried leaf. I unearthed my childhood stamp collection—a shoebox of yellowed cellophane envelopes and old postcards mixed with loose stamps—and learned how to make inlaid cover designs. I cut rectangles and smoothed flat the images of antelopes leaping in Burundi. Neil Armstrong's footprint on the moon fit in a square. The lions and rhinoceros of Mozambique posed in oversized triangles. This is where I had learned the real names of places—Sverige, Éire, Ceskoslovensko, España, and the Republique Togalaise.

I spent days in my house resting and then working and then resting again. I had now spent years in my house being careful with money, with my body. I touched the stamps, especially ones with maps—starred capitals in Cyrillic script, coastlines of far continents. Yellow and green parrots surrounded a little girl in Australia with dark, straight hair like mine pushed back by a blue headband. I used to wear my hair that same way. A smallness spread over this new life I'd made.

My mother called one day. She thought I should get a wheelchair lift van like her neighbors had for their son. She would pay toward it. I found a 1992 Ford Econoline Club Wagon. The owner of the van had died, and his mother was selling it. The woman cried as I raised myself into the air with the lift. The man's sister took me aside, out of her mother's hearing, and told the story of the day four years before when her brother had shown up at her door with the then-new van and yelled, "Drunken road trip to Key West. Get in." And she had.

The van was hard-used and rickety and perfect. A friend ripped out the back seats and put in a platform bed with a six-inch foam mattress. I piled on pillows and hung curtains on bungee cords. I bought a Florida Road Atlas and marked routes that traveled through the back roads of state forests, along winding blackwater rivers, and into mangrove swamps. I went looking for pitcher plant bogs, burrowing owls, crocodiles, malachite butterflies, and crested caracaras. Even without the alcohol, I believe I have honored the van's legacy.

Mosquitoes

The entrance to the campground is guarded by a ranger in a small hut. I stop, turn off the engine, and lower the window. The van takes a moment to rattle its way quiet. My body continues vibrating. It's been a hard drive, but I've made it to the fabled Everglades. Here I am in the paradise of Marjory Stoneman Douglas—the land of crocodiles and pink birds and mangrove swamps once the haven of smugglers. Maybe they still are. Reading that woman's book has seduced me into a yearlong plan that is now unfolding.

The ranger opens his screen window, and we negotiate on a campsite. He says the two campsites directly overlooking the water are taken and will be for the next week. He notices my manual wheelchair in the back of the van and points out a site near the bathroom. They always want to put me close to a bathroom. He says it has a view of the water, so I agree. He slides a screen closed between us, and while he figures out the bill, I read the notices posted on the wall. Below the tide schedule is a board with a stick-on cartoon mosquito. It's bug-eyed and leers. Right now the long nose is pointed at the "TOLERABLE" level. "TOLERABLE" is below "PLEASANT," but above "ANNOYING." There's a level below "ANNOYING," but a flyer announcing bad drinking water blocks it from view until a breeze curls up the edge of the flyer. "DON'T EVEN ASK" it says underneath.

The ranger opens the screen halfway and angles a handful of maps and regulations through the opening. He says, "A warm front is moving in." There's a warning tone, but I figure he means rain. "No problem," I say, "I'm sleeping in the back of my van." He turns away and shuts the screen tight and then slides a second layer of screen over the first. He becomes a shifting, dark shadow behind them. Already on the drive through the park, half hidden in the expanses of sawgrass that murmured with wind, I've seen white lilies and glossy ibis. Wood storks, with their vulture heads tucked into the white fluff of their necks, perched on the delicate, winter-bare branches of pond cypress. Everything is just like in the book. How can I care whether it rains?

It doesn't take any time at all before I'm in my Barcalounger position with my heels propped up on the picnic table and my back slouched against the wheelchair's backrest. A mostly eaten bowl of packaged macaroni and cheese rests between my breasts. Palm trees sway overhead, and I can smell salt off the Florida Bay. A flock of egrets skims the treetops. I know they are egrets because as part of my preparations, I taught myself that necks curled in flight mean egrets. Marjorie's evocation of the Everglades is all around me. Or perhaps I now exist within the covers of a book. Then the bathroom's air dryer roars, and the door clangs open and shut. This is why I don't like camping next to the bathhouse.

Three mosquitoes land on my pants leg and hold their own against the gusts of wind rippling the fabric. I brush at them, and when they rise, the wind sucks them away. Between my feet I can see dusk and clouds moving in over the Florida Bay. I'm no expert on South Florida weather, but those don't look like rain clouds to me. I chase the last milky pasta elbow up the side of the bowl. The wind pauses for the first time since I've arrived, and I can hear a hum above me. A single mosquito lands on my fork hand at the base of my thumb. Another one sits at the crook of my elbow. The hum is louder. The winds gust again, and the mosquitoes are snatched off my body. The hum retreats. I claw hair off my face and let it blow behind me. The air on my neck is warmer than it was earlier.

There's time for a quick tour before dark, so I clean up from dinner, anchor anything that might blow away and drive the half mile back to the marina. I watch birds gather on a sandbar just off shore: snowy and great egrets, little blue herons, all sorts of terns and seagulls. Towering over the gathering are white pelicans. Nine-foot wingspans it says in my South Florida birding book. They, more than anything, remind me that I've made it into the depths of the Everglades. Each species of bird lifts and hovers and takes its turn to arc into the distance, and soon the sandbar is abandoned. Behind me the gift shop lights go on. Perhaps they have a list of guided trips. I give the door my usual strong yank, but it's heavy and closes against a wheel and wedges my wheelchair into the jamb. The cashier rushes over and shoves until I can pop through. The door snaps shut behind me. The cashier murmurs an apology about bugs and wind and returns to her place behind the counter. They don't have any schedules. I have to go to the ranger station on the level above. I buy a holographic turtle bookmark and a strip of postcards. By the register is a display of bug spray. "One hundred percent DEET" it announces in large, neon orange letters. I'd studied all the bug spray offerings at Walmart before I left. DEET had warnings about its ability to dissolve plastics. That seemed too harsh to put on my skin. Walmart also offered a "natural solution." If it'd been in a health food store, I'd have thought it was probably no more than wishful thinking. But Walmart was selling it, so it must have had an effective poison of some sort included. I bought that one.

The cashier lets me out past the door and points me at the steepest ramp I've ever seen. I zigzag around the concrete flood pillars hoping for an elevator, but I end up back at the bottom of the ramp. It has a railing. It has a landing half way. I back up and rush the ramp. I shove my wheel rims hard and then again and again and feel the blood pump through my muscles as I strain forward. Then my arms yank away from the wheels because of the stabbing. Mosquitoes have swarmed my forearms. I grab the railing to stop my backward skid, but my momentum is gone. The offices might even be closed already. I let myself roll backward at a safer pace and swerve from side to side as I take turns releasing a wheel to shake an arm free of the swarm. At the bottom I'm back in the direct path of the wind off the water. The mosquitoes disappear.

At the campground entrance, the ranger hut is abandoned for the night. The leering mosquito has been moved down to "annoying." The dusk is taking a long time arriving, so I slip the turtle bookmark into a mystery I'm reading and prop my feet back on the table, facing west this time. I'll watch the sun set over the bathhouse. The air is thicker. The wind continues but with less energy, and between each lull, batches of mosquitoes hover close. It's time for the repellent. I dab it on my exposed skin. It smells like oranges. The wind drops, and I hold out my arm for a test. Mosquitoes move in like a crowd at happy hour. I shake my arm until they lift off. The repellent might need time to soak in. While I wait for that to happen, almost without being aware, I develop a steady rhythm of hand motions: brush at ears, flap along neck, rub down arms, pat hips, wave at ankles, and then up to the ears again. Waiting doesn't make a difference. There's not much wind now.

Despite how warm it's getting, I put on a long-sleeved shirt and am able to delete the rub-down-arms part of my routine, but I still have to rush the cycle. Wherever my clothing pulls tight over my skin, I feel stings. I pour repellent on my hands and rub it over me as if it were lotion. I increase the speed and forcefulness of my hand motions. While I'm flap-flapping at my shoulders, two parallel lines of stings burn along the top of my feet. I have shoes on. Are these Everglades mosquitoes powerful enough to poke through shoes and the underlying socks? I look at my feet. At each eyelet of my sneakers, a mosquito is curved with her head sunk all the way up to her eyes. That's another fact I learned from my preparation. Only female mosquitoes sting. They need blood to reproduce. Right now, I don't care about mosquito babies. I break routine to press the flat of my hand against each shoe, and blood smears over the white laces. I straighten the tongue underneath. Mosquitoes take advantage and swarm my neck. I roll backward until my feet drop off the table and smack down onto the footrests. I have to make a quick stop to the bathhouse, and then I'll shut myself away for the night.

The bathhouse door is as heavy as the gift shop's and the effort of pushing it open keeps my head bent until it has shut behind me. No other person is here. Gray light filters down from the high open spaces between wall and roof. Silhouetted, unmoving, a thousand mosquitoes hang in the air, legs dangling. Another thing I know is that mosquitoes are attracted by the carbon dioxide of exhales. I hold my breath and close myself into a stall. The room starts to vibrate. On the toilet I keep my pants tucked up and my shirt pulled down, but before I can finish peeing, I'm bit in a ring around where my butt meets the seat. I end up spanking myself. Gasping for breath, I snatch my pants back into place and fluff my shirt out away from my body. Brushing my teeth seems foolish, but I'm going to risk a quick hand washing. I lean over the sink and splash water over my face and neck. Mosquitoes are forced up my nose. I snort and rub at my face. I feel little dead bodies on my cheeks. Live ones replace them, and I slap around my head. This protects my face, but it means I can't move the chair, and a wild claustrophobia rises inside me. After a last flurry of hand motions, I grip my wheels and push out the door like a racehorse.

I bolt for the campsite. The process of opening the van doors, unfolding the lift, lowering the lift, getting on the lift, raising the lift, folding the lift, and closing the doors is slow. When the last door smacks shut, my accompanying mosquito cloud is closed up in the van with me. It's hot. I turn on the battery-operated fan. I aim a flashlight beam at the far wall. Some of the mosquitoes follow it. For no good reason that I can think of, I slather repellent over all my exposed skin before I slide under the sheet. Mosquitoes buzz at each ear in a range of octaves. They spread down my body. I flap the sheet so they can't poke through to my legs. It's hotter. I pat water over my face and arms and hold the fan close. The mosquitoes retreat. I can't see them, but I know they are nearby. I'll read to take my mind off things. I hang the flashlight over my head and hold the book in one hand and the fan in another.

A manly firefighter and a smart aleck yet feminine police detective are standing over grisly remains and discussing splatter patterns when I have a bad feeling. I peer over the top of the book and into the shadows. They are waiting. They clutch to the curtains, the sheet, and the ceiling where their bodies cast elongated shapes in the dome of the flashlight light. One flies at my ear. I hit it away and keep reading while my peripheral vision tracks for any mass mosquito movement. On my next visual sweep, I can tell something's wrong. It takes me too long to notice that the entire curtain contingent has disappeared, and I'm not quick enough to prevent a coordinated strike where my toes are pressed against the covers. I snap the sheet and the mosquitoes scatter. I feel stings on my temple and at the base of my thumb. Why there, why always the base of the thumb? I rub the mosquitoes away. I know better than to start slapping myself again. That way lies frenzy. But something has to be done.

I start with the ones on the ceiling. It works best to smack an open palm against the ceiling and pull. It makes bloody streaks. The more I kill, the more of them move out of the shadows to take their place in the light. I smash and smash until only the mosquitoes that huddle in dark corners survive. It reassures me to think I'm smarter than they are. I wet the edge of yesterday's T-shirt and wipe blood off my palms. I shake flattened corpses off the pillows and flip them off the sheet. I know there are more of them, a few at least, but I'm exhausted from the effort, the long day's drive, and repressed panic. I lie down and cocoon the sheet around my face and make sure the fan is blowing over my head. I turn off the light and wait. And think. What if I didn't pack more batteries for the fan? Will these last the whole night? No mosquitoes attack, but I hear a descant tone over the sound of the fan. I track it to the cracked-open windows in the van's back door, beside the bed. I risk turning on the flashlight. Mosquitoes lie like fur over the screen. They test, probe, and search for weakness. One of the windows has a screen that doesn't fit right. I unwrap an arm from the sheets and snap the whole window shut. Then I snap the other one shut as well. I tell myself that there is plenty of air in the van. I turn away from the windows. The travel clock beside the bed says seven o'clock. That's twelve hours until dawn. I think now about how old the van is and how the rubber around the windows has hardened and crumbled in places. Sometimes water leaks in. Water drops are bigger than mosquitoes. Nevertheless, I fall asleep.

Her gait is rough, something between that of a football player and a toddler. She rocks from side to side as she stomps along the concrete path connecting the marina and the gift shop. The swinging arc of her breasts stirs the air around her. The German tourists with their skim-milk skin and the yacht owners with pressed white shorts and leathered faces can't see her as she passes them, yet they pull away, buffeted by the smell of dried-over sweat and swamp water. The uniformed rangers, the older ones, know she's there but look aside. Her hair is a long tangle of sun-bleached green. Faded rags swirl around her body revealing thick calves and arms layered in loose fat that shudders as she walks. No one sees her face.

She rips open the door of the gift shop and leaves it hanging off a hinge. She's a blur down the aisle toward the counter as customers, for reasons unclear to them, jump for the walls. Stacks of folded T-shirts topple. Pens with alligators painted on the side, panther coloring books, and manatee earrings scatter over the floor. A rack of note cards spins. Over the counter a hand comes into perfect focus. It seizes a tub of the 100 percent DEET.

I wake up. Sweat is dripping down the sides of my body. The sheet is wet underneath me. A single mosquito buzzes in my one exposed ear. Before opening my eyes, I beg the clock to say five or even six. It's two. I'm not sure there's air here in the van. Is my breathing getting weird? I put my face near the back window, crack it open, and imagine millions of molecules of oxygen rushing in. The waiting hoard becomes agitated as I exhale. I close the window, pause, and repeat. Even with my face pressed to the open window, sweat drips off my temples and into my eyes. It stings. If I make it through to morning, I'm going to find a pay phone, make hotel reservations somewhere, spend the day exploring on the road out and be gone from here before dark. It doesn't matter how much it costs. It doesn't matter all the effort it took for me to get myself here. I'm done with the Everglades. Damn you, Marjory Stoneman Douglas.

A lifetime later it's six. Six counts as morning even in the pitch dark. I put on pants and tuck them into my socks. I add a blouse, pull a hat low and load my pack with binoculars, a bird book, and water. I slide onto the wheelchair and position it in front of the side doors. I press the switch that flips them open. Cool air sweeps over me. The mosquitoes aren't gone, but they're less determined. The clouds have passed. I perch on the still-raised lift and look at stars. They are thick in a way that seems like a dream from childhood. My hands sweep the mosquitoes from around my face in a casual way.

Beyond the campground, over the bay, the first bare shades of daylight spread into the sky and blot the stars at the horizon. I lower the lift and roll toward dawn. Checkout isn't until ten so I have this time. My eyes adjust to the intermittent lights of the campground, and I find a path along the shore. It curves back away from the water, but I stop and maneuver as close to the edge of land as I can. Mangroves grow out of the tidal muck in front of me. Mosquitoes settle in around me, and my hands splay and twist above and around my body like an Indian dancer. This disturbs the mosquitoes off my skin. Pink and yellow brighten the sky, and flocks of ibis in black silhouette (necks stretched straight out) fly out of the sunrise until they dip and rise across my path. I hear the rush of air over their wings. Another ribbon of birds arrives close behind, and this time they pull me in their wake. I bounce over a rooted trail that leads into a circle of cabins. Here, people with blue-black skin unload from a van. They carry buckets and mops and spray bottles. They say good morning to me and then resume their quiet conversations in French. Another rush of wings spreads around us. The birds fly over our heads and then off to the main road. Now that I'm back on pavement, I push hard and fast enough that my front casters rattle. I arrive in time to see a line of white wings dip over the trees and into what I remember is a pond area.

I have to take a more roundabout route than the birds, but I find the opening to a path that circles the pond. On the small island in front of me hundreds of white birds preen, squawk, and negotiate branch position. I've found the ibis. My arm muscles quiver from the chase, so I maneuver down an embankment to a bench where I transfer onto the wood seat, put my feet up on the wheelchair, and settle in with the binoculars around my neck and the bird book on my lap. Other early-morning birders appear and climb the stairs to an observation deck. Their conversations drift down along with the smell of coffee.

"Charles and I live south of Corpus Christi."

"Oh, Texas. Bill and I were there last year. We managed a ringed kingfisher sighting. Bill, Bill, turn around. See his T-shirt? I had his life list printed on it for his birthday. Three hundred seventy-one and counting."

"I'm surprised you didn't see a belted kingfisher too. It and the ring are pretty common in Texas. Now the green, that's rare. Even Charles and I have seen it only a dozen or so times. Charles?"

"Yes, dear?"

"What is your number these days?"

"Eight hundred and twenty-three."

I roll my eyes and shift to the far end of the bench. I have to see what these couples look like. They're white, of course. All four of them have harnesses strapping their binoculars against their chests. The guys are erecting scopes. The second woman is exclaiming on the wonders of Costa Rica when a flock of pink birds flies over. The conversation stops and the whole group, including me, lifts our heads to track them.

"Flamingos!"

"No, no, unlikely. They're roseate spoonbills."

I silently vote for the scarlet ibis I've just seen a picture of in the bird book. The angle of the morning light shifts, and the birds turn into another batch of ibis. Above me, no one says anything.

The island is in full sun. The grasses directly in front of the bench rumble with croaks. Sections shiver, rattle, and grow still again. I point my binoculars here and there and sometimes catch a glimpse of webbed yellow feet or the bob of white tail feathers retreating. I hunt for birds until my arms won't hold the binoculars up anymore. My eyes adjust to regular vision and right here, on the closest patch of muck, is a tiny brown heron. It extends its body taut and nearly horizontal. It inches one leg forward. I flip through my book, which I thought I had thoroughly studied before I left home, but I don't know this bird. Just as I find the heron section a voice in my ear says, "Least bittern, dark phase."

I hear a swoosh of movement. The whisperer and two other people crowd onto the bench with me. Hushed words float around.

"Where?"

"Oh, I see it."

"Show me, show me."

"This makes it three hundred and seventy-two for me."

I glance behind me. People are four deep and crammed close. Binoculars angle over shoulders.

The furtive bird moves into the underbrush. I follow it, unblinking, with my binoculars and watch it clutch to the side of a grass blade, raise its head to match the angle, and blend into invisibility right in front of my eyes. It's almost embarrassing how excited I am. Perhaps I should start a life list. The crowd moves on, and I pan the other patches of muck looking for what I can't see. A black bird floats out into the open and lets loose with what sounds like the opening guitar licks of "Wipe Out." I open the book again. It stays visible long enough for me to teach myself the difference between immature gallinules and immature coots. It's all in the flank feathers.

I would like to stay on the bench forever, but I'm hungry. I keep the binoculars around my neck just in case something amazing appears. They smack one breast and twist around the other as I shove back up the embankment, and I find myself thinking about a harness. Following the ibis has circled me almost back around to the campground. It's only a short trip on smooth pavement away. A truck towing a boat, another one pulling a collapsed pop-up trailer, and an ancient Volkswagen van are the first in a long line leaving the campground. It's worth checking whether the two bay-front sites are available, so I rush over the pavement, smacking hard into and over the speed bumps to get a good angle of view across the campground. The sites are empty. I need to grab them before someone else notices. Instead of going to fix breakfast, I add myself to the line. I sit modestly in my wheelchair in front of an RV bigger than my last apartment and behind a Toyota sedan top-heavy with gear. It looks as if they just threw everything up there. The line behind me keeps getting longer. If they have this much turnover daily,

I feel for the rangers. But it's not long before I'm the happy owner of a new, paid-out-the-week, site assignment. I'll move the van and then have breakfast sitting in bed looking out over the bay. The day is mine.

It is only as I rise into the air on the lift and look over the campground, spotting just two other vehicles in that big expanse of flat land, that I remember last night and the reason for this mass exodus. I hesitate. The lift holds midair. I shift in my chair to look at the water. As if out of a mirage, an ancient pirate ship in full sail skims over the bay. Tourists line the sides. Two roseate spoonbills, actual ones—I can see the splayed shape of their bills—fly above the mast. A raft of black-and-white birds fly with their long lower beaks dropped into the water's surface. From here I can't see the red legs or the orange at the base of their beaks, but I know they're black skimmers from my preparation studies. And then, I kid you not, dolphins curve up into the air.

The Everglades is giving me her all, and something inside me wants to match the challenge. I decide the coming night can't be as bad as the last and that I won't even look at the leering mosquito chart anymore. I will buy more batteries.

I continue my ascent into the van. A gust of salt and humidity buffets against me, pulls my hair. Eyes behind my eyes blink, and I smell muck and armpits. "Yes," I say to my dream. "I won't forget." I add DEET to my list.

Negotiating a Life

Decades of oils and care kept my cast-iron skillets seasoned and ready, but they became too heavy, and I had to give them away. I grumbled about the no-stick, probably toxic, insubstantial pieces of crap I used instead. All the casserole dishes were next, even my favorite one. Made out of a cream-colored pottery decorated in a swirl of brown streaks, it had a matching lid with a steam vent. I should probably talk about it in the present tense, as it stays at my friend Aliesa's, and there are Thanksgivings where it's placed on the table in front of me steaming with mashed potatoes. But the dish wasn't mine anymore, which meant I no longer supplied the ubiquitous lesbian potlucks with the best macaroni and cheese in the world or my kick-ass spinach lasagna. Instead I brought olives or grocery-store fried chicken pieces or nothing. At home my cooking became determined by cleanup requirements. Usually I could manage a skillet (the stir-fry), a pot that just needed a rinse (the steamed vegetable), a plate, and a fork. On energetic days it was pasta of some sort, which required a skillet and cutting board (onions, lime, basil, shrimp, perhaps) and two pots, one of which needed scrubbing (pasta water, steamed vegetable), and a bowl plus a plate. Some days had to be simple and cleanup was a glass and a spoon. (Milk mixed with protein powder.) On the impossible days I didn't eat.

It took me longer to figure out housekeeping. Mopping the kitchen floor left me gasping and bent over my knees. I made jokes about watching the floor dry, but really it just took me that long to recover. When once again I was sleeping in sheets smeared with body grease, I sat at the desk and analyzed my budget. I dropped seafood and fresh berries from my grocery list, and I stayed part of a social life by eating before I went out to dinner with friends. "Oh, I had such a big late lunch," I said as I ordered just an appetizer. The saved money was used to hire someone to clean the house.

I got better at imagining possible future limitations and making adjustments early. Papermaking was going to be too hard, I could tell this. I took a nature center class on how to weave pine straw baskets and was ready when I had to put away my screens and paper press. All around me longleaf pines grew in open meadows where sunlight poured through to an understory of wildflowers. I wandered through bog buttons, meadow beauties, and purple stands of paintbrush to gather the foot-long needles. My lap, my hands, my home: they all smelled of forest. Pain diminished, and the desperate fogs of exhaustion descended less often.

I braced the beginnings of a basket between my breasts and held the next layer of pine straw in place. My leather-thimbled thumb pushed long-eyed embroidery needles threaded with dried strips of palm frond through and up and under. I learned the names of new stitches: wheat, diamond, and popcorn. I learned how to twist a row up into a handle that curved over the basket. A fern stitch worked best for those. In small rings I made spokes with raffia the way they do on islands off the coast of Morocco, and I wrapped embroidery thread around the spokes, dropping and adding to form a pattern. The rings added openness to the baskets. And in the stories that I was writing again, I attempted to drop and add words in ways that let light come through.

Binding books still gave me pleasure, but my sense of humor failed. When the lesbian community newsletter collective I was part of wanted to have a fundraising dance, I was the killjoy. I argued that we needed more subscribers to sustain ourselves, not a one-time event, but they were already discussing the pros and cons of a mirror ball. The one of us who was the least likely to actually do anything was making grand plans for a kissing booth. "We'll take shifts," she said. I thought, "You bitch." These women just wanted to have fun, bring fun. I knew I was the bitch. But at a planning meeting for a friend's birthday party, at my writing group, even just deciding among three people which movie to go to, with less and less provocation, I thought, "You bitch." Sometimes my lips moved. Once the woman next to me, whom in a less tired version of my life I was fond of, put a hand on my arm, smiled, and asked me to repeat myself. She was sorry, but she hadn't quite heard what I said.

It seemed best that I stop participating in anything that required a meeting. I retreated into my home and again became selfish of my time. I learned not to promise my future energy to anyone, to say instead, "We'll see," "Perhaps," "Maybe," and "Can I let you know at the last minute?" It wasn't enough. I avoided people the most I could without anyone noticing. Whenever that was impossible—birthdays, Thanksgiving, break-up consoling—I learned to feign interest with a nod and to fake compassion with a head tilt.

I did have a girlfriend during much of this time. It suited me then how little she featured into my figuring out the practicalities of living. It suited me that I took care of her perhaps more than she did me. It suited me to lie in my bedroom unable to move without pain and be hungry and not to call and ask her to come heat up soup. It made no sense to me to have the basics of my life dependent on someone else's availability, goodwill, or whim. It suited me to enjoy each other within each of our limits on intimacy. And we did laugh and often spend nights together, and when my mother was in a terrible accident she drove with me to the hospital, and we liked each other so very much.

One level of fatigue and pain can be put in a mental corner and ignored. Another can rule a life. Each night I searched for a way to decrease my shoulder pain long enough to fall asleep. Left arm up, right braced on pillows, then a flip and reversal of arm position followed by a half-tilt onto my back with an arm laid over my forehead. Sometimes it worked to scooch down the mattress until there was room for an over-the-head, fingers-under-the-headboard stretch. But I woke up and once again, as before, when I was still working, my arms were too weak and numb to push me upright. Once again trapped flat in the bed with a full bladder, I clenched and released my fists and then lifted and dropped my forearms until feeling returned. It was as if I were both in the memory and the right now. I stared at the ceiling and thought about the metal triangles people recovering from spinal cord injuries had over their hospital beds. I worried that "nursing home and bedsores" was not just me making fun of my own anxious self anymore.

I wasn't as afraid this time. In the intervening years, I'd actually had injuries that kept me bed bound, and I'd had pressure sores from sitting. I found out that injuries heal. I'm a practical person. I learned how to take care of my skin. I dried thoroughly. I used creams. I paid attention. Practical solutions, even to emotional problems, please me. I was handling this. Then one day at the library I was too weak to push the wheelchair through the stacks. A sense of the looming apocalypse swept through me.

I decided that I needed a scooter-type wheelchair. Within the year I had one. (That is a simple sentence. It was not simple. It took months of paperwork, appointments, and phone calls where I changed my tone from ingratiating to helpless to threatening, as needed.) At home I still used my manual chair, but I rode that scooter all the way to the library, and men yelled, "Slow down, you're going to get a ticket," and I waved at them and smiled. I didn't yet know that I'd have warnings about the tickets I was going to get yelled at me for all the years of my life.

My girlfriend and I, briefly, were renewed. She bought a house nearby. We both agreed it couldn't be within line-of-sight with mine. Friends—I liked my friends again—loaded the scooter into the back of a car, and we drove to state parks. I went out farther than I ever had on trails where we saw water moccasins and wild bison and watched cranes dance into the air. I was wild and free. I'd made the big change.

I clung to making journals. I found a book on nonadhesive bindings. After hours lost in the ecstatic study of spine-pleats and integrated endbands, I devised covers that attached in puzzles of interlocking tabs. But, despite the scooter, this big change that should be making all the difference, my arms ached more and for longer after each bookmaking session. I simplified the rest of my life. Bookbinding counted more than weaving, so I tried weaving less, but my skill level dropped and this was unacceptable. I didn't see any choice but to hang up my skeins of raffia and put the washed pine straw in plastic bags on the back porch. I threw away the box of metal rings. I bought soy milk and protein powder in bulk and again avoided answering the phone. I planned a rest after cutting each book board to size. After yet another morning of temporary immobility, I dipped into savings and bought an expensive mattress. It helped. All these small sortings of my life helped, but not enough. I needed to "buck up," as it was always called in my family, and make the hard decisions.

Taking off my braces for good, quitting my job, moving—each time honesty had been required before anything could happen. The current truth in my life was that it took too much, it hurt too much to keep making journals. At night, I would think this and then forget it in the morning. Until the day I set down the knife I was using to chop a carrot. I rubbed into my wrist to ease the ache. Out loud this time I said, "I need to stop." As I heard my own words, relief dropped through my body, softening it.

And as always, with this first honesty more became possible. The next truth was that, for a good while now, the creative joy of journal making had been a memory, a desperate illusion buttressed by both hope and grief. The truth after that was much the same illusion. I saw past the hope and grief and left my girlfriend.

I gave away the cutting mat, T square, and bone folder, along with my collection of book boards. The leather thimble was now used only for sewing on loose buttons. The surface of the worktable cleared as the supplies and tools left. I kept the table in place, bare. I told myself it was still good for wrapping presents and ironing. I stopped ironing. I asked a friend to take the table, and when she folded up the legs and walked it sideways out of the house, I cried. For me, over and over, this peeling away down to the truth of a situation is just plain sad. But only for a time.

Each day, many times a day, I passed by the empty space the table had once occupied. I moved one thing and then another into it, but nothing looked right or was functional, and I still called it the worktable area. One day I stopped in front of this empty space. I asked, "What is important?" I knew the answer as I asked the question and rushed off in search of a measuring tape. It wasn't in the toolbox. It wasn't on any of the back porch shelves. I found it in a desk drawer and swirled through my small house's jigsaw of furniture to measure things. I started in the guest bedroom. It had been years, what with front steps and inaccessible bathrooms, since I'd been an overnight guest in anyone's house. Why should I give over so much space to potential visitors? Screw them. I measured the width of the dresser. It would fit into the worktable space. I calculated and mentally rearranged. The double bed could go. Maybe someone would buy it, and I'd get a daybed. The printer could fit on top of the bookshelf. I'd need a corkboard for notes.

It is here in my new writing studio, reclined, propped against a backrest of pillows with the computer on my lap and a yellow pad pinned under a thigh and a blanket over my feet, that I remember the story I wrote in high school, the horror of exposure, the muteness, the inability to hear. I know that I've remembered it before. And forgotten it.

And I remember another place I wrote—a canvas tent on a wooden platform with a ramp built by an old lover, in the woods at the edge of an old soybean field in South Georgia that she now farmed. This tent, given to me by a gathering of friends, so many of whom I now lived among, was a strategy. I figured I could keep working in the bookstore if I had frequent breaks. So I'd put in my regular sixty and sometimes more hours a week for three weeks and then have a week off to spend in my tent. It had a battery charged by a small solar panel that gave light and ran a small fan. It had a real bed and bedside table. In this bed I remembered pieces of my childhood: a cowgirl outfit with a hat, holster, gun, and fringe; a wagon I could make go with my hands pushing a lever up and down. When a lizard ran across the screen of the tent window, stopped and puffed its red throat out, happiness had flooded me.

One night it stormed. The canvas walls shook and snapped and held the rain out, but the inside was thick with moisture. My breath seemed to have nowhere to go. And I remembered the echoing sounds of sea lions. I smelled the seawater and spoiled fish. I remembered being high on my father's shoulders as he walked us into a cave. The rocks bubbled and dripped water. The sea lions' barks and squeals bounced around us. This must have been the Washington Coast, so I must have been two or three. This might be my earliest memory.

Another night, with the fan flipping at the pages, I read Audre Lorde's *Zami: A New Spelling of My Name*. I read how she poured boiling water over her hands in an inexpressible rage. I remembered a decade before, unable to speak about anything really, when I planned, step-by-step, how I would go in the kitchen, boil a pot of water, and pour it over my feet in a way that would seem accidental. Then I would be noticed. I never did this. I was afraid of the pain. The crescent moon, outside the screen door, a few days past new, rose through the tree line. Crisscrossed by swaying branches, it broke into pieces that made shifting shadows inside the tent, on the quilt, over my hands holding the book. Fireflies, as if they were small pieces of the moon, flew close to the screen.

As I sit in this room I've made, this new place to write, in this new century, and am so happy, these memories, for the first time, seem part of something, a thread of my life, a pattern of fear and impending apocalypse before honesty, before change. They've become a folio, a set of pages, sewn in tight to my life.

Dehiscence

I'm not ignorant. I know a body needs touch. I've read about the orphans in far countries left alone in cribs, about failure to thrive, about attachment disorders. Sometimes I measure touch. If a hello hug from a friend lasts five seconds, and if I get four hugs a day, which mostly I don't, that's a daily touch total of twenty seconds. This is meager compared with sleeping beside someone—60 seconds times 60 minutes times 8 hours, which equals 28,000 seconds. I'm not sure how to put the percentage of body contact into the formula, but however you figure it, the results are lavish, and they disquiet me. So I work at becoming more used to touch. At a social event I remind myself to make an effort and swing my body out of the wheelchair and down into the couch. Any concern about how to push back out of the cushions is put off for later, and for two hours I end up rubbing shoulders on both sides, with an occasional brushing of clothed thighs. The math is complicated, but I come up with 7,200 seconds. I also have massages—3,600 naked seconds.

At times I leave a massage with my mind blurred. Sometimes sadness (no, just the memory of a sadness) ushers me out the door. Later, soaking in a tub, the massage oil slipping off my body and into the water, I wonder whether I will have to travel the same looped path again. Will this sadness I feel lead back to an indignant anger over the paucity of physical contact, of connection, of familiarity in my life? Will the anger, this righteous demand for intimacy, lead me back to a relationship? All these changes I've made, have they made no difference? Long ago I quit drinking. I lay awake beside my lover at the time, unable to sleep, knowing that I would end our relationship soon. I wanted something to be different. This time, I had thought, I will do this sober.

Many things did change, but still the pattern, the cycle, persists. There will be the time period of sharing my life with someone the best I know how with the most ease I can manage (in my experience six months at the least, seven years at the most) during which I come to expect daily and exuberant skin happiness. Then perhaps I notice myself not asking for things—please pick up cereal for me while you're at the store or pump the gas or even pass me that bowl—because I know she is tired of me, but I'm still clinging to touch and don't want to be any sort of bother that will give her enough courage to leave. Or perhaps, in another relationship, I think, over and over, "Now. I need to end it now." A return to the desperate quality of loneliness that happens only from within a relationship is an early warning of the cycle moving on. But I continue, trapped in place by knowing the inevitable future. Soon after (in my experience a week to a year) the relationships end, touch is gone, the outrage about its absence slips away, and I reside in the comfort of forgetting. I have lived a productive, engaged, and creative life from this place for many years. And yet I am remembering that there is something to remember. Under my skin, hardened nerves melt. The cycle moves on to sadness and to this return of knowledge.

Movies have sex in them. Sometimes I notice. Sometimes my body remembers a nipple pulled tight by the weight of a belly sliding by, and the way one finger can trace fire down the side of a neck stretched in anticipation. The sun's heat on a bare shoulder recalls a kiss, after sex, when lips become soft and wide. My tongue will press against the roof of my mouth and suck out the memory of tastes and smells. Sometimes I remember all this, but it takes effort. The other intimacies are easier. A friend walks beside me. We're talking about our lives, our mothers, one dead, one still alive, and she puts a fingertip on my forearm where it lies on the wheelchair's armrest. The history of our friendship flows between us through this small point of contact. This touch comforts me. It has balance. I don't tense away, and I don't crave more. (Damn, here I am justifying the way I think things are and will always be. Screw those emotional connections that come from a fingertip, a good talk, a long laugh, or decades of shared experiences. I will make myself crave the huge coming together of skin and the smacking sound of body liquids.)

I was in a bed in the hospital, not my regular bed, so it was most likely a postoperative ward. I was five. I felt something wet "down there." I was sure I'd peed myself and lay quiet, in terror, knowing I'd be found out. The staff in the ward where I lived, had lived for the past many months, was unkind when this happened. Here a nurse looked under the sheets and put her hand, not in a rough way, on my shoulder and asked, not in a mean voice, why I hadn't said anything—not in a real question way, just as something to say as she called the doctor over. She handed him thick white pads of gauze. The next I remember we were in a concrete room with a dome of bright lights overhead, and the doctor was talking to me. He showed me the long black thread. He said my incision had opened up, and he was going to sew it shut again. Nothing he did hurt. I concentrated on his descriptions of knots. He showed me the scissors and told me how many stitches he was putting in as he put each one in. No one had ever explained anything to me before. Even today, it can soothe me to touch into my groin and alongside what I now know is called a dehiscence—a reopening of a wound—such a lovely word on the tongue.

When I was ten, the year I started my period, I wore a corset. It was a hard plastic the color we still called "flesh." Cinched tight with straps and a metal bar across my belly, it sat on the top of my hips and stopped just below my new breasts. On their way to being large, my breasts jutted over the ledge of plastic. Boys pointed and said things I don't remember. A neighbor lady eventually took my mother aside and told her I needed a bra.

The corset was molded to the shape of my body. Here's what I remember about the process of having the mold made: Men are laughing and teasing each other and including me in their fun. "He's losing his hair, isn't he? Tell him, girlie." They circle around my body laid out on a table. One of the men pulls my shoulders back and my arms out. Another lifts my hips up. Another wraps and wraps and wraps strips of wet cloth around me. I am naked. I am a little girl with a mist of pubic hair and those new breasts, and it all feels wild and good.

"For my next relationship, I'm going to have to be disabled."

I say this to a friend. She goes silent. Her eyes veer off to the side. What is there she can say? In a black-and-white photo of me at three years old, I've got small wooden crutches pressed into my armpits where they push up the poofed sleeves of my eyelet and pintucked dress. Right now, on the other side of the restaurant table from my friend, I sit in a three-hundred-pound wheelchair. I've been visibly disabled all my life. What do I mean when I say that this time around, in a relationship, I'm not going to hide?

After we finish our lunch together, I hug my friend good-bye. We've spent the morning hiking the La Chua trail, where we startled alligators off the path and swerved around mounds of bison scat. I've been chatty and laughing and present. My friend still has a day in front of her. She is going back to her job and will fix dinner for her girlfriend. Perhaps they'll try to make the early showing of a movie. Do I want to go with them?

My plan is to go home, take pain pills, and soak in a hot bath to ease my hips from all the jouncing along the trail. I'll take a long nap. I won't have to cook dinner because of the big lunch, and this is a relief. If the phone rings, I'll hope it isn't someone that needs anything from me. I'll watch television without caring for the hours before I get back in bed to read until I fall asleep. The next day I'll rest, and by the time anyone sees me again, I'll be chatty and laughing and present again. Or maybe I'll decide to accept the invitation and join my friends at the movies, so I'll take that extra, ill-advised dose of pain medication and plan for two days of rest afterward. Either way, this has always been my private life. I've never had to explain it to anyone. No one observes or judges or controls.

There is a woman. We've met at a mutual friend's birthday party and laughed together. She calls and asks me out for a coffee, and we both understand that this is a predate date. I say sure. She suggests four in the afternoon a few days later. I say sure. I say sure even though it is smack in the middle of my naptime during a designated day of rest. Already, with my hand still resting on the hung-up phone, I know I've made a mistake. Right from the beginning of any something that might develop, I've compromised myself, given myself away. And this woman has no clue that I have. This scene is melancholic and familiar. Not again, I think, and call right back. I try to reschedule. I don't tell her why. Already, I am too much trouble. I know I sound too intense. I have to talk around the image of the English teacher holding my paper and knowing too much about me. She says she'll get back to me, but she never does. I feel defeated. I don't know how to do this, this new way. At least I haven't failed in my determination to try.

My first massage was in the eighties, when I was between lovers. Everyone was doing it, so I saved up money and got naked under the sheets. Modesty was never a problem for me. I know this is considered a sign of a relaxed and positive body image, but for me it comes from years of forced exposure to strangers in white coats. If I ever do have a moment of modesty, I honor it the best I can. But there was no modesty in me at this first massage.

She started on my back and pressed at the edge of my scapula, between my ribs, and into the always sore place at the bottom of my spine. It felt good the way tonguing against a loose tooth feels good. I wondered whether moaning was allowed. When I turned over, I opened my eyes and saw, more than felt, her pushing into the hard muscle mass of my arm, which had no more feeling than a log of wood. I almost told her not to waste the effort, but she moved to the other arm and, as if through layers of swaddling, I felt the outline of her palm and a slight give under my skin. I closed my eyes. Her hands left my body. I kept my eyes closed. Would she do the chest? Certainly the breasts must get skipped. The belly? I heard the pump and slurp of the massage oil bottle.

My body reacted before I registered the touch. I twisted up off the table until I was bent over my legs, shielding them, with my fingers curled like a tiger reaching for prey. Red filmed over my eyes. I may have been growling. The masseuse had touched the scar on the bottom of my foot. Something, I'm not sure it was pain, spread in waves from even the memory of her touch. When my vision cleared, I saw her backed against the wall of the small, quiet room. "Intense energy," she said.

I have learned to guide a masseuse around my scars—the pulled-tight sheen of skin along my knee, the puckered gathering of skin along the bottom of each foot, and the wide, soft spreading in my groin. The scar that wraps around my ankle like the tendril of a climbing vine isn't visible. I remember when it was—a white inlay with indentations to either side like a zipper. The skin is smooth now and all one color, but I can still trace the scar's path over the bones of my ankle. I follow the tenderness, almost pain, with the tip of my finger. It's still under there, pulling at the hidden layers of ligament and tendon.

Use the flat of your hand here, I say to the masseuse. Don't press hard there, I say. But in this imagining of a beloved (or this intrusion into my private life as I sometimes think of it), I'm inarticulate even in my own mind. How do I instruct? How do I reveal? More than a decade goes by without a relationship that requires me to answer these questions.

May or May Not

I remember always seeing the underneath of things. I'm sitting on a bath rug, and black and white tiles spread away from me and foreshorten into corners. Summer sunlight illuminates the soap smears and family hairs around the claw feet of the tub. It's Norwegian sunlight and has no humidity to blur the edges. Each small hair throws a shadow. The tub is deep, which means high over my head. I don't remember how I get into the tub any more than anyone who hasn't left her braces and crutches in the bedroom and crawled to the bathroom remembers how she got in a tub. But perhaps I pull myself onto a close-by toilet and then swing over to the rounded edge. It's 1966, and at fourteen I'm strong and agile from a life of crutch walking.

I have probably balanced the beers on the back of the toilet. Or maybe there's a table beside the tub. Yes, a table. It wavers into view—a marble square set on turned dowels of pale wood. Is this the same table that came to me when my mother died and now sits beside my bed supporting a water glass, body lotion, and always a stack of books? I do remember the black plug on a chain. And the swaths of precious summer light through the window— glinting on faucets, creamy over the porcelain, slicking the tiles. It must have been a Sunday afternoon. Afternoon because of the slant of light. Sunday because of how my mouth stank with thirst. On Saturday I would have passed for eighteen in my madras skirt from the Montgomery Ward Catalog and gone to bars. I don't remember that Saturday night, but mostly, on a Sunday morning, I never quite remembered the night before, although I would have caught the last before-curfew bus out of the city and not missed my stop. Sometimes I remember a sloppy groping with a stranger in the back seat. Had I met him at the bar? On the bus? Perhaps on this Sunday my lips feel bruised.

I look up blackouts on the computer. Alcohol messes with the hippocampus. The hippocampus is central to the formation of new autobiographical memories. Still, I know this bath I'm remembering is in the summertime because in winter the light had a harder gleam as it passed through frozen glass and lasted only briefly. All of us American military families still tell tales of the blackout blinds we needed in summer to get to sleep. My mother had a story of how she sent my sister and me out the door and off to school in the winter dark and how it was dark again when we got home. So it must be summer, but family stories, even about astrological phenomena, can dissolve on inspection. The internet tells me the sunrise and sunset times in Oslo. Factually, it could have been summer. If so, then perhaps my mother is out on the porch when I lie to her.

Our house tucks into the side of a hill, and the porch hangs suspended in lilac bushes. Their tops form a perfumed privacy where my mother and the other military wives sit with their shirts off, gathering the sun over their bodies, their big white bras glowing as the women smoke. Short glasses of gin and tonic smell of lime. I watch for a while. Some of them wear shorts that fit tight over their hips and rise in a long curve high on their waist. Others have on pedal pushers that clasp around their calves. They lean back in their lawn chairs. Their legs are crossed, and some of them point a foot and swing it in time to the single on the turntable, "Yellow Submarine." Earlier a Johnny Mercer album was playing. They tease and flirt with each other the way straight women will. My mother raises her hand and protests "no, no, no" when they talk of the pilot at the last party who was always noticing when her glass was empty. He's the husband of someone who isn't here on the porch that day. "Those pilots," she says, "they're just full of talk."

I must have wrapped my pinkie and ring fingers in a sideways grip around the neck of the beer bottle and used the rest of my hand to hold onto the crutch. "Mother," I say, "I'm going to use beer to rinse my hair. All the girls in my class do it." I picture her turning to her friends, rolling her eyes, and simultaneously bragging and giving permission by saying, "And she seems to have to use my best beer to do it." She is, of course, pleased that I'm doing something like all the other girls. She can pretend I'm one of them. She doesn't know or pretends not to know about the rotating schedule of girls' sleepovers that doesn't include me or the class-wide parties where I see everyone open their desk and find a colorful, handmade invitation. They wave them around. I open a book and read. Sometimes one of these women on our porch makes her daughter invite me. As an adult, I can imagine the conversation that leads to the resentful, scribbled invitation thrown on my desk at school. I am beyond pride and always go if I'm invited.

But no one else in my class tells her mother she's visiting her Norwegian girlfriends, which is sometimes true, and then sneaks downtown, sometimes with those friends, sometimes on her own, and pretends she's eighteen. The girls in my class would never know to save the last of a toothpaste tube, roll it up small, and carry it in their cleavage to use before coming in the front door at night. Sometimes my father opens my bedroom door to make sure I'm home. "Prepare for inspection," he calls out. "Yes, sir," I say. One night I'm in my slip, the toothpaste still perched there, forgotten. He sees it and says nothing. The girls in my class probably have fathers who would have asked about the toothpaste, made a scene. Sometimes I pass for twenty-one and am let into the hard-liquor bars. A man will offer to buy me a drink. I ask for a gin and tonic.

The women on the porch laugh, and ice sounds against glass as they drink. I turn away and swing through my crutches carefully so as to not dislodge the two other beers fitted behind my underwear's waistband. My bedroom is just on the other side of the living room at the foot of the stairway. I close the door and unwrap cramped fingers from around one beer's neck and fish the others out from under my dress. I drink one right away. My thirst settles back down inside me.

I do remember the stairs, but it is always the deep part of the night in my memory. I've made the mistake of having a glass of water too late or perhaps dinner was saltier than usual, and I can't wait until morning to pee. I crawl up the stairs backward, my elbows bent behind to lift my body. My nightgown stretches out beyond my feet until it's draped over the smoothed wood and chokes against my neck with each slide of my bottom over a step, each bump of my heels. Midway, on the landing, I pause in the darkness before starting the steep rise to the second floor. At the top I crawl past the snoring of my father and then the silence behind my sister's door. Sometimes she climbs down the fire ladder to roam outside at night.

So I don't remember crawling to the bathtub on this day. I don't remember how I brought the beers with me. I remember the hot water, the bubble bath, and my body swirled with steamy iridescence. Iconic memory, echoic memory, haptic memory—visual, aural, and tactile—researchers have words for it all—the yeasty beer sweating in the steam, the glass cool against my palm. I tilt the bottle over my head until I feel beer against my scalp.

I work it through my hair so the lie will pass inspection. Then I lean against the sloped back of the tub and finish the bottle.

Alongside the beer waiting on the table that may or may not be there and may or may not have become my bedside table, is my mother's razor. She has forbidden me to use it. I'm too young, she says. My mother and her friends have legs that look like silk as they move easily among each other. I prop a heel against the edge of the tub. I lather the length of my leg and shave for the first time. A tendril of blood curves down from my knee, but a quick swish of the razor clears the evidence from the blade. I splash the blood and loose hairs off my leg and inspect it in the sunlight. The scars of old surgeries shine brighter next to the bared skin. The twist of a lower bone makes a different pattern of light and shadow than the legs that flowed up into shorts. I rub along the new smoothness of skin, and it is like silk. This is how it would feel to touch one of those women's legs. This is how it would feel to someone touching me. I open the waiting beer and let the now warm, copper-colored liquid slide inside me. A whisper from the future murmurs gentle, blurred words that I can't understand, but it comforts me that there is a future. I tilt the bottle and drain out the last of the beer. I put it back on the table that may or may not be there and soap my other leg down to where the water line circles my thigh.

Atlanta–2007

I'm older now than the woman I saw leaning against the wall of a building that no longer exists. Much older. The Sears building has been converted into condos. I drive past them and hurry to the freeway. I've been in Atlanta visiting my mother and helping her with doctor appointments and pills, and now I'm yearning for home. I intersect the street that leads to the fabric store where Ms. Garbo's used to be. It was my first bar. I walked into it alone, and then a woman bought me a drink. Sheba's and The Sports Page are gone as well. After a long drive, I pause at my front door. In the window beside it, my image wavers over a glimpse of desk, warm orange walls, and a flower of stained glass given to me by a lover from a quarter of a century ago. No woman waits on the other side, her hand raised, our images mixing through the layers of reflection. This is not that type of ending. I lean a shoulder against the door and go inside.

The Last Period

The tent is set up. I've checked twice to make sure the kayak is secure. I've eaten soup and carrot sticks and an apple and rinsed the pot. For the first time since five this morning when I hefted a bag onto the handle of my wheelchair and my hand gripped the front door knob and hesitated, I stop plotting out what comes next and then next. I sit spread-legged in front of my tent and scratch through my hair, through the sweat on my scalp, and stretch the ends up off my neck. Then I take a foot in each hand, cross my legs underneath each other and rock over my hips from side to side to flex my spine and pull feeling back into my backside.

The Okefenokee Swamp is loud at dusk. A pig frog grunts. It's as if he's sitting on the wooden platform beside me. From the thicket of willows a catbird sounds like the cry of a child's cheap baby doll. A kingfisher chitters across the open water. In the distance, an alligator bellows for his mate, and around my head, a muscular orange dragonfly darts and dives in a hiss of wings as it hunts the first mosquitoes of the night. A train echoes along the edge of the swamp. Throughout this long day sudden sweats of anxiety have overridden the joys of sunlight and swamp and frogs the size of fingernails perched on water lily leaves.

I've made this trip before but never alone. As I paddled the seven miles to the camping platform, I didn't worry as I maneuvered past a green snake wrapped into an overhanging branch. There was no sudden stop or gasp when the nose and eyes and rugged back of an alligator rose up in front of me. Instead my paddle froze mideffort as I tried to remember whether I'd brought the hook I might need if the water levels were too low and the platform too high above the boat. How would I grapple my way up onto it without the hook, and who was I to think I could just lock my wheelchair in the van, crawl to my gear-heavy boat, scrape down the concrete ramp into the water and just do this?

The water levels weren't too low, I hadn't forgotten the hook, and now I'm fed and prepared for bed. This time between day and night is free of anything next to do. I hold on to my ankles and lean backward and let my eyes soften into a wide and blurred field of view. What has been a ruffling breeze strengthens, and I lean forward again to scan for clouds whose bottoms hang low and dark. The sky is clear. I do hear the kayak slap against the wooden supports. I scoot to the edge of the platform and lie flat out on my stomach to reach over the edge and yank on the bowline. It holds fast, but I tie yet another knot. When I sit up again, my clothes are stuck skew-whiff over my body. The evening is still humid. The moon is rising. The last of the sunlight sheens over the grasses and turns each patch of water into a pink pool.

The coming night air arrives in fits and starts of coolness. I undo the buttons on my shirt to feel more of it on my skin and keep going until my shirt is off and pinned under a thigh to keep it from blowing away. The bra is next. It is only now, with the wind wrapping around me, that I know I can take off all my clothes and could have hours ago, ever since the campers from the night before passed me on their way out. As the full moon clears the horizon I'm sitting naked, cross-legged again, on the still sun-warmed wood. My inner lips are spread and pushed under me. They feel too large. I reach down to adjust, like a man, and my hand comes away bloody.

All day, as my hips tightened and then melted open, as my breasts hurt each time I bumped them, as the now explained waves of fear rose and fell, I didn't think of periods. It had been three months. I was fifty. I was done with that. I told myself the knot of pain in that space between butt and back was because of the hours of paddling. With my bow tucked into a rare patch of shade, I'd twisted a fist into my spine as I stretched forward to peer at the spiky, miniature wildness of sundews. I straightened to touch the long, translucent tubes of pitcher plants. These plants exist and thrive in what scientists call a "nutrient-poor" environment. Nothing around me looked poor or deprived, although the patches of soil seemed as if they would scatter apart from the wake of my kayak. The water was clear. I had splashed it over the back of my neck and face and licked my lips—no algae, no minerals, no salt. Pitcher plant flowers grew on separate stalks higher than my head, and I reached to put a finger into the petals. The thick yellow of them lit up my nail.

Now in the moonlight, I stretch over my head again, and the knot in my back releases, and fullness spreads down into my thighs. I've thought this before and been wrong and yet, as the songbirds quiet and the first owl of the evening sounds, I'm certain that this is, at last, my last period. This particular constellation of sensation is visiting me for a final time. It's been forty years.

I had my first period when I was ten, as did my mother, and as did her mother. So I'd been given the talk a few months before it happened. I was climbing the steep staircase of the split-level with one arm stretched forward on the banister and the other using a crutch to lift my rear end and braced legs up to the next step. My skirt bounced out and high. My seven-year-old sister was below me. "Mommy," she screamed, "Sandra's bleeding." My mother gave me a sanitary belt with toothed metal triangles that hung back and front. It tangled with the panties and ankle socks in my underwear drawer. It would be another year before bras were added to the mix. A cabinet was cleared out in the bathroom vanity and loaded with stacks of pads so wide and thick and that it seemed like a magic trick to fit them up between my legs. The cabinet door was to always remain shut. I was to scrub out any bloodstains before my panties went in the hamper. Sometimes I didn't. It was my rebellion against this unfair burden of stratagems and secrecy. I'd pretend I forgot when my mother whispered her accusations. But she didn't tell my father. Secrecy, it seemed, had its uses.

From the first and then forever, I had cramps that made me whimper and gasp, and sometimes the metal triangle on the backside would smash between my skin and the high thigh band of a leg brace. But I'd already lived through hospitalizations and surgeries and knew that pain wasn't something that had a solution, and it was best to ignore it. I knew how to get used to things. I adapted.

In my elementary school, if you started your period, your mother had to tell the staff and then you weren't allowed to use the students' bathroom during your "time." Instead you walked down the long hall to the front office observed by group after group of whispering girls and confused boys. There you used the secretary's bathroom. On the walk back, sixth-grade girls snickered at the crippled, new-to-the-area fifth-grader. I heard the words "faker" and "stupid" hissed behind me. More than once I delayed the walk of shame until I bled onto my dress and had to pretend I hadn't for the rest of the day. Pretending wasn't hard. Ignoring the girls wasn't hard. Stares and whispers weren't new. I could make the world go silent. I'd see mouths move but not hear the words.

We moved again, and I went to a new school. By this time, I'd acquired the management skills needed. I knew to shorten the back tie to compensate for the pad's tendency to jut forward, and I could wiggle a sideway drift back to center. I figured out that if I bent forward and twisted, the metal part would sometimes pop up out of my skin. Best of all, more girls had become part of the club, and the special waste receptacles showed up in the student bathrooms. I was back to being as invisible as I could ever manage, although I never saw anyone else lean into a wall, curve her body, and pant through the high arc of a cramp.

I embraced the stick-on pads. They were harder to control, but scrubbing the bloody underwear was worth the pleasure of throwing away the frayed elastic belt with its evil triangles. We moved again, and traveling was easier with stick-ons. At my mother's childhood home in London, I was introduced to the hush-hush menstrual routine. They had an outhouse. (My dead mother, in a shrill voice, is now instructing me to make it clear that it was not an outhouse. It had plumbing. It was built on to the side of the house. You just had to go outside to get to the door.) An outhouse would have been easier. Instead, in the privacy of a narrow hallway, my mother instructed me to wrap the used pad in toilet paper and slip it to her in the kitchen. She was appalled when I tried, in front of my grandfather, father, and sister, to discreetly hand her something that was almost the size of a shoebox. I may have overdone the toilet paper. There must have been a code of conduct because the men pretended not to see anything. My sister did take a breath to speak, but my father gave her that look, and she shut her mouth. My mother handed the now-invisible menstrual pad with its mounds of toilet paper unraveling here and there to her mother, who laughed. The men still didn't look up from their soft-boiled eggcups. My grandmother opened the door of the iron stove sitting in the middle of everything and tossed the pad onto the waves of orange flame. She latched the door closed with a clang. Everyone ignored the sparks and burning blood smell. In that kitchen, reality was whatever my grandmother decided it was.

Tampons existed, but we teenagers were, of course, not allowed to use them, what with the risk to our virginal hymens, although that was never said directly. At my high school graduation, I decided to try one. There I was, already in my white gown, in a stall of the girls' bathroom for the last time ever, and an experienced tampon user was giving instructions from the other side of the door. I failed at the first attempt. She handed another paper-wrapped tube under the stall. It hurt since now I know it was inserted only partway, but that's how I walked up on stage to get my diploma. I don't have one of those looking-back-in-retrospect-from-a-place-of-maturity explanations for this. It just seemed like something I had to do. In college they came out with the bullet-shaped tampons that opened up inside you like a parasol. They excelled at being small and convenient, but they could get lost. One day a guy and I planned a sexual romp. Beforehand in the bathroom, despite leaning against the wall to wedge my shoulder forward to lengthen my arm so that my hand could reach farther down and up, my fingers just couldn't get a good grip on the slippery string. So I climbed into bed with the guy, where he'd been waiting, and presented the choice—leave, or find it for me. Young men will do anything for sex. But that was the end of the bullets.

Which was fine because the bleeding was coming harder and for longer. I went from large to super to extra-absorbent, and the companies kept making whatever it was the tampons were made out of better at wicking up liquids. If I timed the end of my period wrong, my insides would rip a little getting that too-dry, mystery of corporate design out of me. Menstruating women started having sudden, desperate illnesses. They labeled it toxic shock syndrome, and the way I was scratching up the sides of my vagina made me susceptible. It's odd to read an article in the paper with a list of causes and dangers and nod yes and then yes and then say out loud, "This is exactly what I do." It's like being shouted at. I was stunned that I—who was by now a vegetarian and recycled before people recycled and was a member of the first organic food buying club in Atlanta and a lesbian who questioned all things male—was allowing these dangerous, dioxin-bleached, penis-shaped products of corporate greed anywhere near my delicate, most womanly tissues. I rushed to the local co-op and bought a set of cloth, reusable pads. A belt came full circle back into my life, but this one had loops of soft cotton.

What with the bucket sitting by the toilet for the presoaking of used pads and watching blood swirl around the sink as I rinsed and squeezed and rinsed and squeezed, I was now more in touch with my bleeding. This was an aspiration of many of us lesbian feminists of the eighties. Women saved their blood and buried it in their gardens. We got on all fours and did the special stretches that were sure to harmonize our bodies into a crampless state. If that didn't work we took dolomite, a mixture of calcium and magnesium. Some wore T-shirts that said, "I am woman. I bleed for days and do not die." Every twenty-six days for ten days I passed clots the size of blackberries and enough blood to fertilize acres. I tried Midol and Tylenol and drinking. The much touted superdrug Advil had just been released for over-the-counter use. I took higher-than-recommended doses of everything. Nothing helped. Pot made it worse. I wanted a T-shirt that said, "I am woman. I bleed for days and want to die."

In the nineties I decided to go back to tampons mostly because I had started kayaking and needed the convenience. Also, you didn't hear about women dying of toxic shock anymore. They had to be safer now, I told myself. But in your forties the media, your friends, your doctors, and the actual reality of increasing risks for this and that cause fear. Ovarian cancer is scary. It has hardly any useful symptoms except for breakthrough bleeding. I started having that. Every month I had that. Even I, after a year, when for a short while I had decent insurance, decided it might be best to have things checked out. The gynecologist, who despite his designer suit looked like a fourteen-year-old boy, told me what the problem was and that it was completely fixable with a laparoscopy. It turned out he was completely wrong about everything he thought was going on, but he did find endometriosis all over. He burned it out of there. During the postoperative appointment, he said it was odd that I hadn't been having pain from it, maybe for many, many years. I said, well, yes, I've always had pretty severe pain with my periods. He said that it would have been nice to know that. Which I thought was a snippy comment but probably came from his defensiveness about being wrong about everything.

Still the laparoscopy was a success. These winding down years have been a comparative joy. For the first time in my life, the phrase "mild discomfort" has a meaning beyond irony. Advil, it turns out, is good for something.

The moon is overhead now. The mosquitoes are descending. I go into the tent, fold a bandana into a pad, put on underwear, and pull the waistband as high as it will go to hold everything in place. I've brought pain meds, but a shade of my eighties self says to wait. For a last time, during these hours filled with the chuffs and scurries of night animals, I'll feel the tug and stretch inside me, the rise and fall of pain.

In the morning I make an emotional return to the present with a handful of pills and muttered goddamn about having to scrub blood one more time. I check for alligators before I swirl my underwear into the water. Blood curls into the swamp. Rooting around in the dry bag turns up another bandana and more underwear. The used bandana goes in the trash container, and after I break down my campsite and paddle away, there's a pair of rinsed-out, beige cotton panties draped over the kayak's bow to dry.

The morning sun and night dew have combined into a glisten that clings and drapes over surfaces. Everything looks labial to me. The rose pogonias shake their pink, frilly lips. The water lily blooms unfurl. Flashy blue damselflies spin past in jeweled bracelets of mating circles, and I find another species of pitcher plant whose burgundy, decumbent leaves spread wide over the fragile soil and are veined through in a darker red. I spend a long time looking down at them, touching along them. When sandhill cranes trumpet nearby, I look up and around for the first time in a while. The kayak is drifting into a large lake I've never seen before. I'm possibly lost. I'm possibly lost in a 43,800-acre swamp. Older friends have spoken in despair of the brain fog that comes with menopause. Has it arrived so quickly?

I retrace my path in a sprint until I find the exceedingly well-marked trail that I missed. I park myself directly under the sign.

Eventually I stop panting and regroup by eating the remaining apple before I go on. Five hours later, the clear water thickens with minerals and the detritus of living things, and the thin patches of earth rise into banks.

I'm in a zone of transition, an ecotone, where pitcher plants mingle with nutrient-loving purple iris and white hatpins that sway on their leafless stalks. Soon I'll pass through to where lush walls of wax myrtle and fetterbush line the path, and later palm trees, and then cedars and oaks and pines will tower up from their rich soils. I pause and look back over the wet prairie. Ecotones aren't just a mosaic of the habitats to either side. They harbor plants and animals unknown to either one. The butter cream blooms of swamp bays send a lemon sweetness over the water. To this world on the edge, the in-between, my body contributes the smells of sweat, apple, and the final overflow of a now-soaked bandana.

Immoderation and Excess

It takes a year, but I wrest a real power wheelchair from Medicare. The half measure of using a manual wheelchair with a scooter backup has stopped being sufficient. This is the change that has been needed for a long while. The special backrest, the butt-cradling cushion, and the big batteries that go forever mean everything is easier, and everywhere hurts less. My world expands. I have dinner parties again.

Each time I buck up and make the big change, my reward is a dinner party. The dinner party's extravagance of energy and time isn't available for long, but I make the most of it. I start setting the table a week ahead. I polish my mother's silver. My grandmother's decorative spoons resting in their satin-lined boxes are placed at the ready. At each setting, I put one of the enameled blue bowls from Norway. I gather a bud vase, a platter, a table runner—all gifts from friends and old lovers. I welcome my guests to a table infused with many kindnesses and memories, some of them mine, some from a past unknown to me but nevertheless present.

I also start kayaking. I know. What an expense of muscle strength. It isn't practical, but it is possible and oh, it makes me happy. Kayaking brings me new friendships. My kayak—yes, I buy one—is carried out of the store and pushed into the back of the van, where to my delight it fits into the only space it can lie in and still leave room for my wheelchair and allow the doors to close behind it. I didn't plan this, I didn't measure or calculate.

It just worked out. And it works out that listening for the gulp of baby alligators, the huff of a manatee rising, or the high trill of nesting eagles brings a new shape to my writing. It becomes—for me—rowdy, and travels to farther reaches.

Looking for the V

Withlacoochee River—North Florida
Full Moon Weekend
Water Levels: 54.94, 54.39

"They're having a fight," Alice whispers into the dark car where Jackie and I are sitting. It's six in the morning. "Should I offer to separate them?"

I'm not sure. Who wants to start a camping trip riding with the pissed-off half of a couple? But Jackie leans across me and gives Alice a hand pat and tilts her head. Alice nods. Their fifteen years together has just allowed them an entire conversation.

Alice walks back to the other kayak-topped car with an offer to switch places with Beckie or Madeline. Alice can attest to the value of this technique and not just because she's a psychologist. On our last camping trip as a group, it was Madeline who reported that Jackie and Alice were yelling at each other in their kitchen. They chose to separate themselves for the two-hour drive, that one to the St. Mary's River, and by the time we finished loading the gear into the boats (a task that can be delicate for an off-kilter couple), all was well.

This time Alice returns alone and wedges into the pile of drybags, coolers, and life vests in the backseat.

"They said that they're fine."

"Oh yeah, fine, right." Jackie and I mutter the words in unison.

"Do you think I should go ask again?"

"No, no." Jackie lowers her voice and adds, "We could give them the name of a good therapist and leave them." We laugh the guilty laugh of friends of quarreling couples everywhere. "But really, can we go now?"

Here is the part of the trip where Jackie is impatient. She doesn't want anyone to take that last bathroom trip, chat too much, or look for their sunglasses. This morning none of that happens, and within a quarter of an hour we've left Gainesville and are headed north on I-75. I adjust the passenger seat, put my feet on the dashboard, and think how being a single person has many pleasing moments. I have a code for them in my head: "Happy, happy," I think to myself.

Before we reach our exit, they already have to stop for gas. After corralling everyone into cars, it is never a good idea to let them out, and, sure enough, everyone scatters. Except me, since my manual wheelchair is buried in the trunk under the rest of the gear, I don't want to do anything to slow us down even more, and I don't have to pee anyway. Madeline taps a Candy Red nail-polished finger on my window and waves as she goes by. I tap my Baby Peach polished one back. Our home spa date was weeks ago, and they're a bit chipped. I see Beckie on the far side of the cars. She's using her height to reset the kayak ropes.

Eventually, everyone is back in place. Alice and Jackie say they didn't dally, but there must have been some wandering down the aisles since they report to me on a variety of Florida souvenirs, including the dried-alligator foot backscratchers. They have also bought more coffee, which only leads to more bathroom stops. This is the part of the trip where I become irritated. I practice breathing deeply until we're going a satisfying sixty miles an hour.

In our car the *Big Chill* soundtrack is playing, and we dance in our seats to '50s tunes. During the slow songs, we discuss the perennial camping questions: If we can hardly find room in the car for all this gear, how are we going to fit it in our boats? Where is the cooler, and can we start eating now? And does that left rope look loose to you? We decide it doesn't, and I relax into our consistent forward momentum.

Reading from my slip of directions, I direct us off the freeway and over to the County Road 150 bridge where we slow to see the river for the first time. I lean out the window and look into patterns of reflected light and shadow. It smells green and wet, and my heart invents its own skipping pattern the same way it does when a handsome woman leans in close. It's hard to leave the river, but a mile later we arrive at the meeting place for the shuttle service.

Jim the outfitter is waiting for us and has a million river details to share. Everyone else leaves the cars to find a bathroom, while Jim leans on the car door beside me and talks. I'm surly because I'm still stuck in the car, but I remember my responsibilities as trip planner and make myself listen. It's obvious that he loves this river. I find my map, and he shows me where things are.

"Go to the right at this shoal, to the extreme left on that one. Here's where the power lines cross seven miles down. Three more curves in the river, and you'll see a good camping area on the east side."

I make marks on the map.

"I could put you in a little north of here—it's closer but steep. Maybe we should go to this other one, or there's this real easy one, but it's a few miles away."

I'm thinking: shut up, take me to the closest place and throw me in.

"Well, Jim, that first one sounds just fine."

My weak-bladdered friends herd themselves into cars, and we follow Jim down a sandy trail on the northwest side of the bridge. It's not long until Jim pulls over and stops. I look out the car window at a fifty-foot drop. The river's edge is thick with cypress knees and brush. Jim leans in my window again.

"Now, there's this other place we could go look at and then come back here if we want to."

"No way. I mean, I'm sure this is good."

Jackie has clambered partway down the hill.

"No problem, Sandra. We can get you down fine." She's a midwife and thinks anything is possible. Neither of us cares if she's lying.

Everyone starts throwing things out of back seats and trunks. My wheelchair reappears, and I'm finally free of the car. I turn my chair so I'm backed up to the drop. I lean forward over my knees, brace my arms against the sides and wrap my fingers around the footrest tubing. I am locked in. It's understood that Beckie will back me down the hill. She's the athlete and always knows exactly where her body is in space. And I've known her for twenty years. Jackie moves behind to help, and we start down the hill.

Midway, my right wheel runs high onto roots, and I'm dangling sideways, strands of my hair sweeping along the ground. I mention, maybe in a loud voice, that if they can't hold on to let me know. I want to have some control about how I fall before the chair goes over. Beckie assures me, maybe also in a loud voice, that they've got me, and the wheels bump off the roots, and the chair levels again. I think I hear "drama queen" muttered. When we reach a small, flat area a few feet above the water, I let myself fall onto the soft sand.

The wheelchair is whisked up the hill and folded into a car. Alice and Madeline are going to follow Jim to the take-out ramp, which he assures us is paved, and drop off the cars. Everyone helps bring the kayaks down, and I get my first good look at Beckie and Madeline together. Their faces are tired and post-crying, but they are sweet with each other. Nevertheless, as the cars leave, I'm glad that all couples will be separated for the kayak-loading phase of the trip.

Jackie comes down the hill with life vests in each hand and paddles sprouting at all angles from under her arms. Beckie follows with dry bags perched on each shoulder. They surround me with piles of stuff and are laughing as they tromp up the hill, arm in arm, for more loads. I start strapping, snapping latches, and hooking on the bowline, seat, and paddle leash. I listen to the two of them go on about their girlfriends.

"Look, she's packed this plastic in plastic."

"Oh, that's nothing. Here's an umbrella—no, I'm wrong, two umbrellas. We already have three ponchos. What is she thinking?"

"Five gallons of water!"

"We have a rule about this—if you don't use it on a trip, you can't bring it on the next one. I'll never have to see these umbrellas again."

"Did we each bring a full set of cookware?"

"Where am I going to stuff this pillow of hers? Really, a pillow. On a camping trip."

I tighten the strap over my big dry bag with the two pillows in it and think "happy, happy." Scooting to the water's edge, I calculate which cypress knees I can squeeze between.

"Can one of you push my boat down to me?"

Beckie steps close and squats to control the slide of the boat into the water. I lean one hand on a cypress knee, pivot off the bank and land in the center of the kayak seat. After arranging the binoculars around my neck, I tighten the paddle leash and squirm to get the seat just right. Then I put the paddle in the water for the first time. I'm floating. My shoulders fall away from my ears. All worries about water levels, weather, and camping sites dissolve into the current. I look at the bank where my friends are bent over their boats. I love them, I love everyone. Gently back-paddling, I hold still in the stream flow. I don't know what's past that first curve, but I reassure myself that I've done every bit of planning and research that is possible. Now, there is only the river.

I spin the boat and paddle upstream while I wait on everyone else. I stop at the bottom side of a set of shoals. They look manageable, but I've never been in any rough water before since it's not something we have much of in Florida. I've read books and know you're supposed to look for the "V"—whatever that means. Jim the outfitter said this stretch of the river has a set of Class One shoals each mile.

I hear a car engine downstream and paddle back to the launch site. Alice and Madeline are waving good-byes to Jim. I watch them slide and skip down the hill where they immediately reorganize how their respective girlfriends have loaded their boats. I stay out of hearing range, but the tones of voice stay amicable. Soon boats are going in the water, and I let the current take me. Jackie and Alice are next. Beckie and Madeline stay behind, kayaks close, talking.

Since the drought, our Gulf rivers have been low and slow, but not here. It's been a long time since I've had the luxury of a strong current. The banks are high, wooded, and empty of people. The sun is a gentle heat over my shoulders. We're passing through a patchwork of state forest and privately owned land. The private lands are obvious because of the cows that stand huge in the water as we float past, their eroded paths to the river scarring the bluffs behind them.

One by one we hear it. Jackie cocks her head, and Alice shrugs her shoulders at me. I think it's a road, but I can't find one on the map I have strapped onto the bow. It gets louder, and I'm thinking planes or tractors when the water ripples all around us. It's the shoals. Alice goes first, while Jackie and I hold our kayaks in place and watch. She bumps up and down, lurches once to the side, and she's through. I square my shoulders, paddle hard and look for the V. For ten seconds I'm surrounded by rocks and swirling cowlicks of water. I never see a V, but I make it anyway, and at the end I raise my hands and take a bow, accepting the accolades of my admiring friends.

While we wait to make sure Beckie and Madeline are successful, Alice decides it's snacktime. First snack and first lunch are my responsibility. I always bring boiled eggs. They aren't fancy, but they're a perfect protein boost, and I present them with flair by peeling each one and passing it over with a portion of salt mixed with hand-ground pepper. As much as it gives me pleasure to serve women in this way, I have another motive. I think traceless camping means traceless, and annoying bits of egg shell can tempt even the most conscientious camper to toss them overboard despite the foreknowledge of my judgmental stare.

After eggs, we are a lively group of paddlers. Madeline and Jackie are laughing together. Beckie compliments Alice on her shoal navigating and then brings her boat alongside me. We try to remember where this river comes from—somewhere in Georgia, Tifton maybe? Alice speeds ahead to look for the next shoal. Beckie follows. Jackie drops behind to take photos of the walls of exposed limestone, and Madeline and I paddle beside each other, comfortably silent.

We continue to see no one. I look over, and Madeline is naked and in the water. She's like one of those two-year-olds who, every time you turn your head, strips down and leaves a trail of discarded clothing. Soon I'm surrounded by bare-skinned, cavorting women. I have on pants, a long-sleeved shirt, a sports bra, and a wide-brimmed hat. I'm not modest, but I burn easily. I decide to get wild. I remove my shirt and slide into the river mostly clothed and still fully hatted. After finding a submerged rock, I sit on it chest-high in the water. Madeline floats by with only her toes, breasts, and face visible. Jackie is swimming across the river, showing white buttocks and an occasional kicking heel. Alice wanders the shore in her sandals, bending over to look at butterflies on blooms. And Beckie, Beckie still isn't all the way in the water. She's beached her boat and has ventured in only calf-high. As usual, she is immersing herself at an excruciating pace, holding her arms stiff and straight with fists clenched, grimacing and then squealing as the water level reaches each of her tender parts—or as she calls them, her "important stuff."

Jackie returns, and group consensus thinks it's time for lunch. I've brought homemade pimento cheese and fresh-baked onion bread along with celery and carrot sticks, apples, and a Scharffen Berger bittersweet chocolate bar. Everyone says it's my best pimento cheese ever, but they always say that.

I tuck away our remains, and each woman wanders over to her kayak and pushes off. We're quiet as we paddle intermittently and take the kayaking equivalent of a nap. It's difficult to tell mileage because of the current and no roads or bridges to serve as markers, but it's a twelve-mile trip, and we're supposed to find a good camping spot at eight miles. When we pass a sandbar, segments of the group think that this is the place. I'm tired as well, but I know we haven't gone far enough and override them by continuing downstream. They have to follow. So much for consensus.

When we hear the loudest roaring so far, we all hesitate until our boats come up even to each other, as if we were at a starting line. One by one, we sit straighter, tie down water bottles and grip our paddles. Alice sprints ahead, pulls over, and slides out of her boat to walk past the shoal. She's scouting. She returns to her boat and paddles to the extreme left. She makes it. Jackie's next, and she hits something hard and jerks sideways, almost overturning the kayak. I go, avoiding Jackie's route. Water is flipping over itself in all possible directions, and everywhere I look there are flat, angled patches. Are they the famous "V" shapes or the tops of rocks? It doesn't matter since the boat is being pulled, pushed, and twisted, and paddling is a joke. At the end, I am shoved sideways into a calm spot. I take my bow.

It's late afternoon when we go under the power lines. The river curves three times, and on the east bank is a sweet sandbar. We start to unpack, and my life goal has become to get the air mattress inflated, take off my wet clothes, and lie down on my two pillows. Alice helps me, and soon I'm resting as everyone else assembles all their own comforts.

Alice and Jackie have a tent smaller than mine, and Beckie and Madeline have what we call "the little Hilton." It fits their double air mattress with plenty of extra room. Madeline passes by my tent door from time to time. She is stripped again and intersperses her chores with jumps in the water. By this time, it is clear that Beckie is ailing with a sore throat. She wanders slowly, picking things up and then putting them down in other places. When her tent is ready, she announces that she's going to steal Madeline's pillow and rest awhile. Alice is exploring the woods behind the sandbar, but Jackie calls to her, and they cavort in the water, kissing and laughing. They swim to the far bank and climb the bluff, and I watch their bare forty-seven- and fifty-four-year-old backsides bend to climb the narrow path. I think of wood nymphs, Imogen Cunningham photos, and the places in the world where women taking off their clothes can stop a war—their naked bodies the ultimate authority. Madeline alternates between playing in the river and checking on Beckie.

I'm rested enough to be hungry when Jackie and Alice swim back. Jackie starts fussing with her pots and coolers, and I move out of the tent to watch her. Dinner is her responsibility, actually hers and Alice's, but Alice does the cleanup. The meal starts with an appetizer of cream cheese, cocktail sauce, and crabmeat on crackers. Everyone except Beckie gathers around, but a plate is prepared and placed by her sick bed. We are munching, heads bent over the plate, hands reaching for more crackers, when we feel a cool wind. A dark cloud comes fast over the trees and blocks the sun. The wind blows hard and cold, and a few fat drops of rain land around us. Jackie scurries to cover the food, I zip my tent, Madeline gathers her scattered clothes, and Alice gets a gleam in her eye. She rushes to her kayak and returns with the two umbrellas, handing them to me and Jackie with a flourish. Jackie refuses to open hers, but I open mine and huddle under it expectantly. The rain slides by just to the side of us, and the sun shines again. Alice insists that this still counts as using the umbrellas. Jackie groans.

Jackie finishes unpacking her special camping cookware and utensils. She's especially fond of her collapsible spatula. I've had so much good food from these pots that my stomach growls when I see them. Beckie crawls out of her tent just as the asparagus finishes steaming. She's feeling better. The tang of bay and onion hits the back of all our throats, we smell rice, and soon I'm leaning against my kayak and eating shrimp jambalaya out of a plate propped on my belly. I pause intermittently to moan words of appreciation. Jackie is perched behind her stove, Alice is handing around food, and Beckie and Madeline are seated on their life vests. By the end of the meal, I'm listing sideways, and they are lying down, life vests now serving as pillows. We don't sit up again until Jackie heats the lemon sauce to go over the gingerbread she has unveiled from the bottom of a cooler.

After dinner we talk about how good the meal was, Beckie feeling better, the moon rise, and what to do with food scraps and grease. Alice says bury them; I say pack them out. Beckie also says to bury, but above the high water mark. Madeline says isn't that the moon between those trees, and why does it look bigger sometimes? Jackie thinks it's because the moon is closer to the Earth. I say it's only an optical illusion caused by seeing it low in the sky with trees and houses in front of it. Someone says it's because really the world is flat. Alice experiments, holding her thumb in front of the moon and squinting. She says when it's higher in the sky she'll see if it's still thumb-size. We start measuring things with our thumb. It seems that with this system Madeline's tush, the sauce pan, my tent, and the moon are all the same size. Alice points out satellites and planes and names planets.

When the moon shines on our tents we go to bed, proud that we've stayed awake until past eight. I hear extended goodnight kisses from Madeline and Beckie's direction, and farther down the sandbar Jackie whispers, "No flashlight? We have all this crap but no flashlight?"

During the night, as usual on these trips and despite my air mattress, stabs of shoulder pain wake me. I sit and rub my shoulders and pant and worry about the long paddle the next day. But I stare through the screen and listen to the night river's squeaks and murmurs. When I hear a large splash, I zipper open the door and lean out. The moonlight shows a wide circle of ripples but now the river stays calm. The color-leached brightness along the far bank throws strange shadows. My shoulder is better. I go back to sleep.

The next morning I'm repacked and loaded before the first coffee addict crawls out of her tent. Jackie gets the water boiling, and soon the sound of a zipper comes from the other tent. After caffeine fortification, Beckie and Madeline start breakfast by laying out soymilk cartons in a variety of flavors, since we all, except for Jackie, have entered the hot-flash era. We're in various levels of undress, eating oatmeal, when we hear trucks across the river. Doors slam, voices carry over the water, and there he is waving—Jim the outfitter. He calls out to us over the water. He tells us that this bluff is a popular weekend launch site. We had thought we were in the middle of nowhere.

It's odd to remember that there are other people. After two loads of canoes put in and are carried off by the current, we forget again. Jackie wants a picture of the campsite. She gets naked, puts her camera in a drybag, holds the drybag in her teeth, and swims across the river. She's standing on the far bluff when a fishing boat rounds the bend. Those little electric motors are quiet. When I look from the guy-filled boat to the far shore, there's nothing left but a camera on a tree stump and Jackie's head bobbing in the river. The men are polite. They pretend they haven't seen and keep their heads turned our way and chat about the weather as they pass by.

After breakfast we play. Alice sits on a bent tree trunk in the shade and watercolors; Beckie and Madeline romp like otters, with much splashing and laughing; and Jackie inspects the bottom of her kayak for gouges from the day before. "How thick is this plastic?" she calls out.

Intermittently tents are collapsed and packed. Some of us brush our teeth, some of us don't. I decide I don't have to conserve strength because I'm packed, only have to paddle four miles downstream, and someone else will drive home. I purchased a paddle float after the last trip when a branch tilted me out of my kayak, and I had to have help getting back in. It fits like a sleeve over the end of the paddle, and I blow up the air bags until it's snug. I swim the kayak out into deep water and teach myself how to slide up the braced shaft of the paddle. Soon I'm able to throw myself into the well of the kayak with not much thought required. I'm satisfied and exhausted and wondering how big the bruises along my arms are going to be when I remember the leftover gingerbread.

All I say out loud is "Gingerbread," and Alice lays down her paintbrush to scrounge in the cooler. We gather around the pan. Alice shows her painting, and Beckie reads us a bit of Buddhist philosophy, and then ironically, for me the feeling of endless time ends, and I want to go. I say pointedly that it's already one. I say we don't really know what lies ahead. I say we might have to drive home in the dark. I say, to myself, that I'm being obnoxious and there's no reason I can't go ahead on my own.

I float downstream, alone, calmer. Houses are visible from time to time now, along with more trash and signs of campfires. Before I get to State Road 6, everyone else has caught up. The final miles flow through high, fern-laden banks seeped with water that forms miniature, spring-fed grottos. We develop the skill of listening for the music of water bubbling into rocks. If fairies exist, this is where they live. We pass rust-red rocks carved, inexplicably to us, into massive shapes. This restarts the discussion of how I need to help out and get a geologist for my next girlfriend. (Sometimes a herpetologist is suggested.) We pass a section where choking swaths of an invasive climbing fern line bank after bank. We pass two more springheads, stopping at each for Madeline to take a naked dip. After a final, boat-twirling set of shoals, we arrive at the concrete ramp. Gear is tossed into cars, kayaks are strapped in place, and we are on the freeway.

It's dark when they drop me at my house, and I am out-of-my-mind tired. I put on Aretha Franklin and wander from room to room. I wipe down the binoculars, wash water bottles, and empty the cooler. I open mail, listen to phone messages, and make a trip to the hamper each time I find another piece of dirty clothing. On the porch, I unstuff the wet tent and drape it over the railing, releasing a shower of sand. Exhaustion has me feeling drugged and feverish. During my bath, the hot water stings my arms—my moment of partially undressed abandon has led to sunburn. As I brush my hair, I look around and realize that everything is either put away or ready to be washed tomorrow. I go out into the night and the still-full moon. I slap the tent and listen to the next layer of sand fall onto the wood deck.

Happy, happy.

Yielding

Where am I in this story? Oh, yes, I seem to be lonely, untouched, and at a threshold of yearning. Does it ruin the scene or undermine my credibility to mention that as I write, a warm dog is lying between my legs with her chin over my shin and her hind legs pressed against the opposite thigh? Until recently, I'd never had a pet. I gave up houseplants decades ago as I made choices within limited energy. I still think of that huge schefflera. The woman who adopted it named it after me. Is "Sandra" still alive? How did I end up with a dog?

Two years ago, when my mother was dying, and before I figured out that nothing I could do would change that, my days were an anxious mess of caretaking. I had so little experience with caretaking. I kept wanting things for her—a good day of playing bridge, morphine, a cheeseburger just the way she liked it, no more hospitalizations, the right type of candy on the trays in her little room, the right type of bird food so woodpeckers would come to her window, another course of steroids for her breathing without the nuisance of a doctor's visit. She was living close to me for the first time in twenty years, she was dying, and my life was an exhaustion of details.

At night, too tired to read, too tired even to watch stupid things on television, I'd roam the internet looking at dogs available for adoption. I knew this was because I'd lost my mind. Was I to become another aging single woman who had dogs to hug and call sweet names instead of developing a real relationship? There I was on a Saturday night watching videos on Pet Finders. "I'm

Trixie. I love playing hard and need somewhere to let myself go." And, "Call me Dahlia. I'm a shy girl but a cuddler once you get to know me." That's when I saw her. I called a friend to intervene.

"Are you looking at those dog porn sites again?" he asked. He sounded pleased and had me send him the link. The next day his wife and I and their dog (any future dog of mine's best friend) went to the pet rescue place. On the drive home, the two dogs curled together on my friend's lap. This was my first terribly unwise choice, a fit of impracticality, in these long years of carefulness. But my mother was dying, and all my rules seemed wrong.

In despairs of exhaustion, I've counted each time I had to pull myself from bed to wheelchair because of this dog, each time I've had to bend over, each and every time my rest was disturbed. But I've never added up the monetary expenses. What is there to do about those? Does dog touch, dog companionship, dog love—mine for her and whatever it is she has for me—count as real? I think so, but it's different. I don't know how to calculate it. Does it keep me from trying for a human relationship? Am I now officially pathetic? I don't care. Most mornings, once I let her know I'm awake, she stretches her whole seventeen pounds over my chest and belly, and all I see are dog nostrils and ears. I scratch along her ribs the way she likes. She turns over, and now there's an upside-down dog head nuzzling under my chin. She sneezes into my face, and each day I'm laughing before I even sit up in bed.

And here I am again, settling for something less than human intimacy, something other than sex. Or perhaps I'm not. I learned to care for my mother before her death, and I am still learning to care for this dog. Some days I think these lessons have led me down a new path. I've become accustomed to offering daily kindnesses, to giving and receiving affection, and together the dog and I have learned how to play. In dog training, no matter what, you can't be angry, ever. Recently, as usual, I forgot what I had gone back into a room to get. Instead of ranting at my stupidity, I used my dog-training voice: "Just think about it. You'll remember. You're a good, smart girl." With my tone of voice, patient breaths, and my selection of words, I'm choosing not to be angry—truly not angry. This is not a squelching or a concealment or another unvoiced moment. When I lean to fix the dog's bent-back ear, and she nuzzles into my hair, something soft and loose rises up from under my skin.

When someone gave me a digital camera with a flip screen, for the first time in my life, it was possible to move the camera and not my body to get the image I wanted. This instead of putting down the camera to grab up both crutches (or later tapping the joystick) to move a half step to the right, refocus the camera, and repeat until the image was perfect. I took this new freedom and became obsessed with being the best photographer possible. A golden lizard on the chipped blue paint of my house's windowsill, the long line of slats and rails of a beach ramp whose far end had been swept away by the ocean, the blurred orange of rattlebox moth wings hovering over a Spanish needle bloom in perfect focus—I learned about color balance, framing, pattern, texture, and depth of field. When the next level of accomplishment meant the expense of a fancy printer and a better camera, I took stock in a way new to me. There was a choice to make. The photography books told me to exclude everything not directly contributing to the image. Photography, I decided, didn't occupy the same place inside me that writing did. But instead of locking down the lens cap and removing the batteries and maybe even giving the camera away, I decided that photography could just be fun if I let it. An image didn't have to be perfect to hold a memory or evoke the wonder of a moment. And the money I'd thought about spending on a large-format printer, I spent instead on a writers' conference. Composition, focus, the contrast between dark and light—I learned more about how to make what is in my mind exist on a page.

The dog and I also go to classes. She is now included in the composition of my life. The classes teach me how friendships can take many forms. My dog friends (friends with dogs) and I, we cheer the wild child of a Labrador when she sits, just for a moment, on command as much as we celebrate the elegant, composed boxer's three-minute down stay. We discuss remedies for hot spots and fear of thunder and laugh about half-eaten squirrels left on the kitchen floor. When one of our dogs gets cancer, we text and call our concern most every day. We ignore each other's opposing political bumper stickers with a careful delicacy. We are seldom invited into each other's homes.

To be invited into someone's home. Sometimes, in the past, before I used a wheelchair, my apartments were accessible, but that was by accident. Mostly they weren't. How have people I've known who use wheelchairs negotiated their relationship with me? All the years after starting to use a wheelchair but before having a dog, I blundered around about friendships and not being invited into people's homes.

At first, I had friends from before the wheelchair. Some built ramps, and our friendships waxed or waned for their own reasons. Others, for birthday dinners or other traditions we had shared for years, moved their events to a restaurant, but this wasn't sustainable since, eventually, everyone wants to entertain in their own home. It was as if I were a child back in the hospital as I noticed the whispers or sudden silence in a group of friends. It always felt as if I'd been slapped. I waited. Pretty soon, maybe weeks later, or sometimes a whole year, someone would let it slip. "Remember those lemon bars," or "Wasn't that funny the way . . ." they'd say about a housewarming, New Year's Eve party, Thanksgiving potluck, Christmas Eve drop-in, graduation celebration, or game night that I wasn't invited to.

Sometimes people try a direct approach, but still, they're screwed. They'll say, "You know how much I value your friendship" and then come right out and explain that while they certainly would invite me if they could, given the circumstances, of course, they can't, and that I should know how much they will miss me being there. It is a cruelty of conditionals.

I never say "Get a ramp, asshole" because I can still remember the time when I was like them and might have made those same evasions. I do learn to anticipate what comes next after any initial proclamation about our friendship and am already detached before they say the rest. And I wonder about the people who detached from me, what might have been, what I've lost without knowing. I feel this present loss and those past losses, the ones I'd been oblivious to, in a flail of emotion.

It is having dog friends that teaches me to organize friendships in a way that works. I now name people as my writer friends, artist friends, part of my lesbian community friends, or neighborhood friends. The qualifier in front of *friends* frees me to find a place to put these people in my life and find a way to enjoy them and have fun without expectations. It's an emotionally clean place.

But intimate friendships have intimacy. We throw open the door to each other's houses and yell a hello. Or we rush over in the middle of the night to be there, make coffee, or cry after bad news. We will show up to let the dogs out when there's a delay at work. Sometimes we sneak in a dozen cupcakes, chocolate filled with cream cheese frosting, and leave them on the counter just because. Intimacy includes the bedside comfort, delivery of prescriptions, and restocking of the fridge we provide to each other in a time of illness. These are my friends with no qualifier.

But the system has flaws. Sometimes a friend will move, and the new place has steps. Or I'll meet someone new, someone interesting, and ignore the future certainty that at some point, if I can't get in their house, it's going to go bad. Or I believe too soon when someone describes with great enthusiasm the ramp she's going to have built, and then time passes, and I come to understand, usually before she does, that it's just talk. I will never leave cupcakes on her counter, so I assign a qualifier to our friendship. The system works, but still I have to break up with her in my heart.

I've become a writer who sends her work out into the world. Anonymous form rejections with faded ink on narrow strips of cheap paper come back in my self-addressed, stamped envelopes. They don't mind saying no to the crippled woman if they even know that's what they're doing. I am encouraged. I'm that little girl again in the pool, my coach's voice a vibration in the water-distorted air. Sometimes my writing is accepted. The first novel, after a more than respectable number of rejections, is put away. The second one, I think, this is the one. It comes close and fails over and over. Through it all, most mornings, I show up to write. This rigor, just on its own, gives me a sense of worth in the world.

Diana Nyad decides at age sixty-one, two years older than I am, to swim from Havana to Key West. She enters the water on this day when I've been thinking about yearning and being alone, a day when I'm thinking about failure—lack of success, not achieving the desired ends, a decline in strength, being insufficient. It's that one, "being insufficient," that weighs on me. I've become skilled at detaching from my submissions. I write them the best I know how and send them to the appropriate venues in the appropriate manner, and that's no small accomplishment. But today a rejection has snuck under my ribs and sits heavy against my lungs while I consider the possibility that my writing is (that I am) insufficient.

I go to bed thinking that at least Diana Nyad is out there swimming an impossible expanse of water, in the dark, with sharks and stinging jellyfish, and she's doing it by lifting and dropping her arm, one stroke after another. I sit up in bed and make a list: add a paragraph to the first chapter of the new novel, finally write the essay about my last menstrual period, revise the story of my mother and the London Blitz. Write one thing after another until momentum is restored.

Diana Nyad hasn't made it from Cuba to Key West. This is the news I wake up to on the radio. After years of grueling physical training, all those people believing in her, all of us watching, and thirty hours of swimming, she left the water. And, of course, she did make it. She inspired people, she pulled together a world community of supporters, and she swam for thirty damn hours. I lie in bed and listen to the rest of the morning news while the dog insists on breakfast by wrapping her paws around my arm and bumping her forehead against my hand. I know I'll keep writing and recognizing success in all its manifestations. But today all of us long-distance swimmers, me and Diana Nyad, we get to honor this particular loss. I put aside my morning list and let the mattress cradle me. The dog sighs and accepts the delay. We get to be sad. We get to yield.

I Am Here, in This Morning Light

Car doors slam, and boat trailers clank by. Couples call to each other. "Don't forget the cooler." "Scrambled or fried?" "Did you remember sunscreen?" My arm reaches from under the sheet and lifts a corner of the makeshift curtain over its bungee cord rod. Beyond the rear window, past a field of tents, a mist-blurred sun rises over the Florida Bay. I drop the curtain. My palms push against the carpeted ceiling of the van, and my head knocks against a side window as I stretch the best I can on the platform bed. This is my fifth morning in the Everglades' Flamingo Campground. With each dawn, sleep coming and going as light silvers and then gilds the water, I've pieced together a plan of how to be out by myself, floating, in that light. Today is New Year's Eve 2009. By tomorrow, 2010, I'll be ready. I slip off the bed onto the sheetrock bucket chamber pot.

Once dressed, I throw open the back doors. This late in the morning only a few mosquitoes follow the light inside. I brace on a window latch and dangle upside down to pull breakfast from the food box under the bed. After slurping protein powder stirred into a boxed milk and peeling a grapefruit, I lean over my feet to open the suitcase of writing supplies, always, on every trip, propped at the corner of the mattress. With pad and pen on my lap, grapefruit sections piled on a dishcloth at my side, I'm ready to decide. A solo, predawn kayak trip—is it worth the effort? Is it possible?

It helps that my camping companions have already left for home. Friends are great, but they want to come with you. Sure, I could say no, but it's not worth the price to be paid in hurt feelings. If I had a lover, would I even have imagined this trip? Maybe a future possible lover would be scared to kayak in the dark. Or she might be one of those hardy kayakers who travel twelve miles out into the bay to camp on desolate, sandy keys, and I would only limit her. I try to imagine a woman who would help me get to the marina and wave as I took off by myself.

The first bite of grapefruit sprays over the yellow pad and wrinkles the paper. I rip it off and start new. Friends have hinted that I'm persnickety and set in my ways. Ex-girlfriends have noted this as well. But I do not want things the way I want them just because that's the way I want them. I have reasons. One joy of a solo kayak trip is that I don't have to explain—anything. There is no negotiation about where or especially what time. There is no need for my lecture about the difference between nautical and civil twilights and how a predawn launch does not mean you leave the campsite, load the gear, or make a last bathhouse trip at first light.

And it helps that I've paddled this trail over the Florida Bay to Snake Bight before. The first time was years ago, not long after trading in my braces and crutches for a manual wheelchair. I was stronger. I could shove the boat up into the back of my van. I can't do that anymore, but now I have a power chair. It can haul things. Still, all plans have more complexity and less physical leeway. Solo trips don't come together for me as often. I've missed the chance to be silent, notice what is around me, and let tangled, perseverating loops of thought unravel. I chew grapefruit and look over the now sun-sparked bay. Flocks of ibis dip and rise in slow waves as they approach from over the water. They fly into the campsite low enough that people duck. A satin sheen of black wingtips flickers past me. I click my pen and write "KAYAK TRIP" in capital letters at the top of the page. I circle it.

Some things I've already figured out. The wheeled kayak carrier I have doesn't quite fit, but I'll make it work and drag the kayak to the marina's ramp with my wheelchair. And then the wheelchair needs to be left out of the way of backing-up boat trailers but close enough that I can crawl from it to the boat. Yesterday, surrounded by the swirl of families from Michigan and Japan and young, tattooed couples from Europe and troops of both Elderhostelers and Boy Scouts, I placed myself here and there around the marina until I found a spot. It blocks a bulletin board displaying faded notices about fish species, but predawn means that I'll be gone before anyone can object. Most of the grapefruit gets eaten while I think about the mile to the marina. I have to figure out whether the wheelchair has enough battery power for the job. I reconsider using the van to transport me, the boat, and all the gear. But at 5:00 a.m. there won't be any fellow campers wandering by to corral into loading the kayak. I could give up on the early-morning launch, lose the light, and not be alone on the water. That scenario repels me, and I'm back to the battery power calculations.

Battery power is elusive and mutable, and predictions of it are always flawed. I put that page aside and instead make a list of objects. My wallet, camera, good pen, I-touch, and pain meds need to be removed from the side, front, and back pouches on my wheelchair and left here at the campsite, locked in the van. An apple, the car keys, and sunscreen go in the drybag. A procrastinating dither over where to list insect repellent pushes me back to the problem at hand. I spit out a grapefruit seed, dry my fingers on the dishcloth, and return to the battery power page.

Okay. The power chair has to be left in the bathhouse overnight for charging either tonight or after the kayak trip. The transfer into my old manual and subsequent push back to the van uses a chunk of my daily allotment of arm strength. Arm strength is also elusive and mutable. After drawing diagrams with directional arrows and route distances, it seems that if I mostly stick around the campsite today, the battery power will hold through tomorrow. This does mean I'll make the recharging trek after the trip when I'm the most tired. So I start a calculation of physical energy with percentages listed for each activity—bathhouse trip (30 percent), launching kayak (20 percent), actual kayaking (60 percent), getting back in my wheelchair afterward (30 percent of my remaining energy)—and stop when, as usual, the math says I should never even get out of bed. I rip and crumble that page.

The last wedge of grapefruit leaks out the edges of my mouth. I can adjust the kayaking route. I'll hug the shoreline instead of paddling out to Snake Bight. I wet down a corner of dishcloth, wipe my hands and face, and list getting someone to help fit the kayak onto the carrier as a chore for today. Outside my van couples are fussing around their campsites. Now seems like a good time. I sweep up the peel, seeds, and abandoned calculations and drop them into the trash bag hanging from the side of the hydraulics. I extend my stretch into the long reach past my feet for the control switches. The side doors open, and the lift unfolds.

On the lawn behind my van, I make a slow show. First, I attach the bowline of the kayak to my armrest and, with a wide sweep of my wheelchair, pull it alongside the carrier. Next, I pause. The other campers, blurred behind screen tents and tinted RV windows, stare. I've spent days turning down offers of assistance with "No thanks, I've got it" and receiving in return some variation of "Well, you're an independent miss, aren't you?" from the rebuffed helpers. Now that I need help, I'll have to make this show a bit over the top. I lift the kayak as high as I can, but as I expected, it fails to clear the sides of the carrier. Both topple away from each other and flop onto the ground. As I reach (with a soft yet dramatic groan) to set the carrier back up on its wheels, there is the sound of a zipper followed by soft footsteps on sandy grass.

"May I help?" The voice is from the Midwest. The man's beard is gray with lingering streaks of blond and has the still-wispy look of a recent retiree trying out a new life. The offer is a combination of kindness and boredom, and I appreciate it. Soon the kayak is cinched into the carrier. He's curious, but I don't tell him my plans. Sometimes word will get around, and an official of some sort will decide he's required to interfere. That time in the Okefenokee Swamp, when the ranger hemmed and hawed but knew it wasn't legal to stop me, I couldn't stop him from sending a motorboat out to check on me. That was the end of quiet and solitude. I experiment with tying a loop of bowline that will lift the nose of the kayak up, but not too far up, when I hook it onto the back of my wheelchair. We, the kayak and I, make a successful trial tour of the campground. The helpful retiree is back inside a screen tent new enough that folds still crease the nylon. I wave at him as I rattle by. He looks up from his folding chair, from his novel, and gives me a thumbs-up. His wife leans out of their pop-up and waves. I go back to the van and rewrite the list in chronological order. Happy New Year to Me. I scrawl the message over the bottom of the page.

At four forty-five the next morning, I let myself get up. I've been awake every hour certain that the alarm won't go off and listening to the weather radio and worrying about the timing of an approaching cold front. I cinch the headlight around my forehead. Light on, I'm reviewing the list. At this stage of a plan, in the moment of execution, it all seems impossible, even transgressive. In an excitement of anxiety and self-sabotage, I will forget sometimes everything or neglect sometimes that one thing that is absolutely necessary. The list becomes my way forward. It reminds me to move the binoculars, sunscreen, car keys, apple, and cell phone from wheelchair to kayak. It says to go to the bathhouse.

The list does not say to remember the toiletry bag, so I don't, but unbrushed teeth will not stop me. The mosquitoes are circling, but I keep in motion. I'm back from the bathhouse at five. The full moon shows a clear sky. The wind is still calm. The trip is a go. The twenty-five-year-old, beat-up crutch left over from my walking days and the extra large vinyl barbecue cover are next on the list. I pull them out of the back of the van. With the crutch braced along my armrests, I hold the slipping folds of the cover as high as I can. I'm almost to the kayak when I feel the pull. My front caster wheel has run over a trailing edge of the plastic. I try to back off, but the wheel flips and wraps a layer of barbecue cover into its axle. A side turn tightens the cover's cinch cord around the wheel. No longer caring about the noise, I throw the crutch into the kayak and brace my ribs on the armrest to lean as far down to the ground as I can. My fingertips reach into the wad of plastic and rope. From whatever angle I pull, there's no give.

 This has not psychologically or emotionally but actually for real stopped me. Anxiety flushes into my still-upside-down head and pools under my skull. It makes me pant. I have become an immobilized source of carbon dioxide, and the mosquitoes swarm. I beat my ears and swat at my nose and eyes. There's a pocketknife in the wheelchair's side pocket. I sit up in the seat to reach for it, and mosquitoes attack the length of thigh where my pants stretch tight. Finding repellent becomes the priority. I can't remember which list it ended up on. My arm twists deep into the back pouch. My fingers scramble through the leavings of a week of camping and locate the tube between a crumbled park map and a black mangrove leaf. I take off the spray cap and pour it into my hands and rub them down my arms, over my ears, and along the part in my hair where the scalp is exposed. Sure, it's poison, but you reach a certain age and the phrase "long-term effects" has less meaning.

The mosquitoes back off. I finger into the pocket and feel past the earplugs and floss. Under the nail clippers is the knife. I flip out each of the choices and decide on the blade rather than the miniature scissors. It won't cut. I try and try, but it won't cut. I'm going to be stuck here with the mosquitoes for hours, until the campground wakes up. My trip is ruined. I knew this wouldn't work. I feel along the blade, which it seems is an emery board. I exchange it for the real knife. The plastic slices away, but the cord still won't unwrap from around the bearings. I stick the knife into the axle and hack. Strands pop loose, fray, and unwind until only threads are left. I finish the fine work with the scissors, and I'm free.

I becalm myself by studying the list. Once I decide that the umbrella and poncho are to be left in the wheelchair's back pouch in case I've timed the incoming weather wrong, everything is loaded that needs to be, and everything is left that needs to be. I'm ready. I back into position at the front of the kayak and lift the bowline loop onto the wheelchair's handle. It hooks on the first try. The kayak and I rattle past what I doubt are still-sleeping campers.

The mile to the marina seems longer than it does during the day. I worry about being late even as I know that there is no late except for what I decide. Still, I push on the joystick and increase my speed. When the kayak pops in and out of a gap in the asphalt, I hear a new rattle following along behind me. I stop and twist in my seat. The bowline isn't working itself off the handle, and the paddle hasn't fallen onto the road. I resume the trip at a lower speed, but something still sounds loose. I recalculate and make myself a deal. If I'm halfway before the kayak falls off its carrier, I'll drag it along the verge. That will still leave me enough battery power to get back in the afternoon. I think.

And now there isn't anything else to figure out. This trip might really happen. I turn off my headlight. The moon brightens the pavement with a gray luster and throws the shadow of my caravan along the grass. We continue at a stately pace. No cars pass. The road surface smoothes as I arrive. I slow and make a wide, careful turn into the darkness under the mahogany trees that line the parking lot. The marina is lit in thick yellow light. I can hear bowlines clang against the dock and smell the salty coolness off the water. I stop at the top of the ramp and review.

The important thing is not to get out of my wheelchair, crawl over the concrete to the boat, and then look back and see the paddle or binoculars or water or drybag or life vest left beside the wheelchair. I position the kayak close to the water. I load and tie down what I hope is everything. I park the wheelchair, perch at the edge of the seat, and think things through one more time. Then I slide down the footrests and drop to the concrete. As my weight is irretrievably pulled down, as my palms and one thigh hit the ground, I hold my breath. This is usually when I remember whatever it is I've forgotten. This morning, it seems, I haven't forgotten anything. And nothing snags or catches as the barbecue cover fits over my wheelchair. The carrier and my crutch tuck neatly underneath. There isn't a rope to cinch the cover with anymore, but I shove the side of the wheelchair with my shoulder until I can anchor an edge of plastic under a wheel.

I've crawled the few feet over to the ramp and am about to make a controlled fall from the ledge into the kayak when a boat trailer backs down beside me. They'll be headed out into the Gulf. I'll never see them. "We can help?" they ask. No thanks, I say, I've got it. But as I use the bulk of my torso to hump the kayak down the ramp, I gather enough of my bad Spanish to ask them what time it is. Seis en punto, they report. I'm early. Or would be if there was an early other than what I make. One more heave and the kayak slides the rest of the way down the ramp. The cupping of water around the keel moves under me from stern to bow until I'm floating. I'm floating. I lift my paddle and tilt one moonlit blade into the water. That possible, future girlfriend is a mirage on the shore. She waves at me. But if she were real, I wouldn't have executed this complicated plan and wouldn't be carrying the confidence of success out with me into the dark waters.

Out in the bay, the horizon has a suggestive strip of gray—nautical twilight. The moon is behind me, and when fish jump, the west side of the ripples flash. Cormorants make frantic take-off shuffles over the surface, and a brown pelican dives smack into the water. Flocks of shorebirds, too dark and quick to see, snap and hum by my side. The horizon releases streams of red and pink over the surface. I paddle toward them. Beside me, the water galumphs into a heave and drop that presses against the boat. I decide it was a sea turtle. As clouds reflect into the now pink water, I try to center myself in the rose glow between the sky above and the sky below. Kayaking into the rose glow seems to be an optical impossibility. No matter how hard I paddle, the reflections are always not where I am.

The kayak slides through the passage between Joe Kemp Key and the mainland before sunrise. Farther out is the channel to Snake Bight, a cove within a cove where roseate spoonbills roost, and below them, on the mudflats, reddish egrets dance around great white herons. My paddle treads water and holds my boat in place as I think that Snake Bight is not that much farther, that the incoming front won't kick up the winds for hours yet, that I'm here and should just go for it. I also remember that I'm pushing to my edge already and that this isn't a marathon. And finally I remember that I am here, in this morning light, on this bay where no direction is second best or less than.

I paddle twice on my right to turn the boat north and close to the mangroved shore. Still I keep watch to the east. When gold shows through a gap in the horizon's cloud bank, I turn my boat to it and stop paddling. This is the first sunrise of a new decade. I think I'm supposed to wish for something. Probably it should be love and not writing career success. So do I just straight out wish for a girlfriend? Do I really want one? Or is it better to wish to give love, to be capable of love, to accept love. Maybe it shouldn't be just a girlfriend. Maybe it should be a wish for love in the world—a peace on earth sort of thing. I'm quoting out of cheesy affirmation books. I stop thinking the best I can.

The sun's lowest curve is still attached to the horizon. It pulls taut and pours orange light over the ocean too bright to look at straight on. Dawn has been wished to for all the years anyone has existed to wish. "Love," I say. The sun will know what to do with that. I put the paddle back in the water and turn north again. My vision smears into wavering black circles with glowing coronas—images of the sun in negative. The spots fade to gray.

Beside me, the shadowed greens of the high mangrove wall squawk and flutter. My pupils regain their size, and cormorants, great blues, and brown pelicans become visible in the twists of branches. Under the lowest prop roots, on a bird-foot-sized lift of mud, a night heron preens her wings.

The tide is leaving, and somewhere along here the water will run out. But these are full-moon tides so I get farther than I would have thought possible. At the place I think of as the secret cove, I hold my paddle above the surface and drift near the opening. Mosquitoes are its first defense, but my clothes are saturated with enough residual repellent to deter all but a few dozen. I don't go any farther, but I don't leave. I haven't been here in years, and still the birds startle out of their hiding place in the same species order they always have. The roseate spoonbills are last. They fly over my head, rippling scarlet to salmon in the new light, pale cherry in their watery reflections. They disappear onto a white strip of beach in the distance, and I follow them. The mangroves recede to reveal marl gray beaches where I imagine crocodiles lay their eggs, and then my keel bumps onto the raised edge of mud left by a tidal creek wandering out of the trees. This is as far as I go. I put my feet up on the sides of my kayak, lean into the seat, and scan the distance with binoculars. What has seemed to be a beach becomes a hundred white pelicans. The roseates are sprinkled among them. I put down the binoculars and stretch my arms high over my head. Breasts lift, a spine loosens, ribs spread wide.

As if there's been a signal, rafts of pelicans lift, extend their nine-feet width of wings, and fly past me. Other flocks—ibis, sanderlings, cormorants, the roseates—go by. They follow the change of tide. I should follow them. I put my paddle in the water, and it sinks into a stir of mud. My boat has been left behind. I rock my body against the kayak seat and take careful backward strokes. The paddle edge only skims the surface until the keel sucks loose, and the rasp of muck underneath me lessens. When the water deepens, and the current turns the boat, I rest the paddle on my knees and let the tide pull me home.

At the point of land visible before I turn back west, I see another kayak. A woman is paddling. Is this my girlfriend, already delivered? We pass, nod, and say good morning. She tells me there are dolphins around the corner. I can tell she's Canadian. That would mean a big commute. Well, she'd have to move down to Florida eventually. I'm not leaving my own home. Which is pretty small for another person. She'd have to get her own place. We continue past each other. Around the point I see the dolphins. The two of them stay close and touch each time they huff and rise. I watch until they leave for open water.

The marina is awake. Boats motor out of its entrance and up the channel. The sandbar in front of the Visitor's Center is above water and crowded with birds. I paddle through the sea grass meadows toward them. On the far side of the sandbar, a ranger is leading the early-morning bird walk from the lawn along the seawall. I hear him say reddish egret and see tourist binoculars raise and point at me. I rest into my backrest and pull out the apple. In front of me the egret lurches through the crowd of white pelicans and black skimmers. It jerks a wing open and shut as it searches for food. I eat my breakfast as the tide lowers, and more wading birds arrive to poke into the almost-exposed surfaces for clams and worms. I tuck the apple core into my shirt pocket. I'm ready to go back.

The wheelchair is still there. This is always a relief. But the ramp is different. Low tide has made it a long, steep way to the top. This was not in my calculations. I paddle hard, lean back to lift the bow and ram as far up the concrete as I can. No more than the tip of my bow sticks. I rest. My muscles are wobbly from the trip. Lots of people pass by. They can't tell I use a wheelchair so they don't stare except in envy. I imagine. I rest and think about how I can do this. There will be crawling. And it will be in front of people, so I'm less likely to feel comfortable or even be allowed to collapse flat out on the concrete partway up. I'm gathering myself to get started when a Spanish-softened voice asks if he can help. I don't even wonder how he knew I needed help. It is not one of the men from before dawn. Yes, I say. Can you pull the kayak up the ramp a little?

Two heaves and I'm at the top of the ramp, past my wheelchair. I have to laugh and wave my arms and say, "Sufficiente, gracias, sufficiente." I roll off the edge of the kayak and over to my wheelchair. Usually in front of people I scoot on my butt. Somehow I imagine that it looks less weird, but rolling is easier on my arms. And really, being stared at is being stared at, so today I roll. And I do that thing where I remove myself. The people around me blur, my hearing diminishes, and I look no one in the eye. It is as if I'm alone. Four full revolutions over the concrete my hips will feel tomorrow, and I'm alongside my wheelchair. I fish the crutch out from under the cover and use it to flip the plastic up and over. And now for its main purpose. I put the life vest on the concrete, twist on to it, and raise into a shaky kneel. I slip my arm into the crutch and angle it out from the chair, making sure the tip is stuck into a crack before I put my other hand on the wheelchair seat. I take a breath and lift, except that I don't. Some weight comes off my knees, enough to make me topple to my butt, but that's it. While I'm leaning against the wheelchair, panting and working harder to ignore the milling crowd, I decide the crutch angle is too steep and that my body should start farther out from the seat. I might have the strength for only one more try. I reposition and concentrate. It's not graceful, but I do get the edge of one butt cheek on the seat. That's enough. I pull and lift until I'm centered. With one finger I push the power button, the controls light up, and it is only now, now that it's done, that I'm certain that this trip is possible.

Once the carrier is perched alongside the kayak, I let myself notice the world again. I smile at the crowd around me. I try to yank the kayak onto the carrier, and of course, fail. But it works.

"May I offer help?" I believe he has a German accent.

"Yes, thanks. The carrier needs to be positioned under where the seat is. Great. Now, let's wrap the straps in front of the seat, and I'll lift the bow while you tighten the heck out of it. No, tighter." I might be sounding bossy, but really, why waste his or my time? We're done just as his group of people starts offering suggestions.

"Perhaps, to slide it higher?"

"Shall I hand you this water?"

I say no to the kayak adjustment, no to the water, and thank them for their help.

"You are the expert, are you not?"

I'm not sure which of them says this or what their intonation means, so I give a generalized bland smile while I think, "Yes, I sure am." I lift the kayak into place behind me and turn in a wide sweep toward the campground.

The road is now full of RVs, trucks, minivans, cyclists, and people walking with binoculars strapped to their chest by harnesses. The kayak and I get thumbs-up, waves, smiles. People yell "Happy New Year" at me. I wish I had a picture. I know I'm looking dang cute. This could get me that Canadian. Sure my shirt gapes over an ancient, stretched-out bra, and my hair is spiky but not in a stylish way. The zipper on my pants twists off over a hip, and I'm not sure I've been remembering about deodorant, but I know from experience that after kayaking, when I'm this tired, my face beams a sort of feverish, angelic glow.

After unloading and reassembling my gear, I lie on my bed with the back door open to the Florida Bay. I've showered. My power wheelchair is in the bathhouse charging until morning. I'm on my bed until I leave to go home tomorrow. I take anti-inflammatory drugs. I don't think about how hungry I am since I'm too tired to reach into the food box. I listen to the weather radio. The front is moving down the state. Tomorrow is going to be close to freezing. Right now, around me, the air is the warmest of the whole trip, and the mosquitoes are encouraged.

Before I have to cover up or close doors against them, the first signs of the coming storm arrive. I lean over to the lift controls and open the side doors. Wind rushes through my van, blowing the mosquitoes away, and I can feel change on my bare skin in the curls of sharp air that swirl through the humidity. People from far away are lighting grills for dinner. People from Florida gather their gear, close their windows, and take down awnings and screen tents. I leave the doors open to the gusts until the last moment. It comes suddenly, the rain. Couples yell to each other about what to grab first. With a flip of the switch, I shut my doors. Rain-blurred images of campers pass by the windows. I'm self-contained until morning.

Pride Goeth

As I approach sixty, all these years of change and rearranging, these sorting throughs of my life, make me think of myself as learned and wise. As friends who have never experienced disability in their own bodies become older, I have words to offer. I give advice about learning the paradoxical dance of limitations that lead to new horizons and unexpected joys. I give examples from my life. I offer solutions to theirs. I chirp with an unrelenting cheer about how my life has turned out.

Some of them complain that, for the first time, they aren't seen as sexual beings. They push with disgust at the loose skin that hangs down from their arms. I manage not to say "buck up." Not out loud, anyway. But I think of how, what with the braces and crutches or now the wheelchair, my body has often been an emptiness in the eye of the beholder. I think the good thing about having been left on my own to fill this void is that set ideas of beauty, of health, of sexiness, and of what a woman or a man should look like have taken less of a hold on me.

A friend rises naked out of a swimming pool and drops of sun-exploded light fall off her sixty-year-old body. It's a friendship of thirty years. I don't think of her body often, but today I watch the twist and rise of her wide, still-wet hips. It's as if I'm watching art move. And that's it, I think, that's what is beautiful to me—the way that on this day, in this moment, her body is her, and she is her body. They inhabit each other fully. And I, in that moment and in many others, believe in my own body: the size 3 baby-soft feet, the polio-altered spine, the lovely sensitivity of my nipples, the place on one hip that always hurts, the breadth of shoulders and softness of thighs, the seldom-seen cuteness of my butt. Sure, sometimes, in clothes, I'm not happy about how I look. A blouse pulls open across my front, pants never fit right, and this dress looks like a tent, but my sexual self is not dependent on an outside gaze. I get to inhabit my body as I please. I watch some of the aging people I know figure out this way of centering desire within themselves. Others become bitter from the loss. Once again I have a sense of being better prepared, more skilled, already competent.

I know that, unlike my mother, I will have no one to figure things out for me. But there never has been anyone. My house is already ramped, and my bathroom has bars. Even during a bout with the flu, with a hundred and four–degree fever, I know to make a plan. "If you are still having trouble breathing by morning," I write on a memo pad, "call an ambulance." I sit up all night, dressed, with the phone by my side, scared to lie down, and in the morning I'm better. I feel accomplished. I can succeed whatever happens. I have this figured out. But now my left arm is failing.

I write with my left hand. I lift my dog's water bowl with it. I use my left arm to slice watermelon and bread. It's one of the ways I touch between a woman's legs, my legs. With every transfer in and out of my wheelchair; onto the toilet; into the writing bed, the television bed, and the bed bed; and then back from these beds to let the dog out, or because I forgot a spoon for the oatmeal, or because I have to pee again, I press my palm flat down on a surface until my wrist thickens and then, as I jam my elbow stiff, I twist my body around a left arm held straight. And it takes both arms braced to lift my whole body up, water heaving and falling, onto the edge of the bathtub. And now my left arm is failing.

These are stark words that may not be accurate. But for no precipitating cause that I can determine, pain travels into my neck, through my shoulder, and divides my bicep. It explodes in my elbow, snaps down into my wrist, and blurs all thought. If I'm chatting with someone, I hang my arm down and pant unobtrusively. Sometimes I hold my arm over my head. Sometimes people notice. They say concerned, kind words that require me to blink hard and set my jaw to keep tears back. Just needed a little stretch, I will say. The attack passes. I rejoin the conversation and cover the best I can for what I've missed. I'm sure I say something inane.

Perhaps this is an injury. Injuries can heal. But if it is an injury, it's a stubborn one. My grip is weak. I don't lift glasses with my left hand. I can no longer pull a comforter over my shoulder or rearrange a pillow with my left hand. Some days, between the times I need it, I cradle my arm into my lap and let it rest there. It seems to me the pain hovering around it must be visible. It hurts to sleep on my left side and on my right side and especially on my back. Stomach sleeping has always hurt, since within an hour something in my spine locks up, but I'll take that hour and the extra one where exhaustion trumps pain. Taking off a sweater or pulling on pants is hard. Lifting boiling pots of water filled with pasta should be out of the question. The basics of daily life are once again no longer routine.

The old fear is back. The apocalypse is nigh. I'm in the abject terror stage, and it's hard to think in practicalities. I do go to the acupuncturist more often. She looks at me, head cocked, and says, "You know this will get better, right?" I believe her. I'm so relieved. But the rest of that day and the next and for weeks and months after, my arm hurts more than ever. A masseuse works on my arms and shoulders and neck, and I fall asleep on her table. Sleep is so precious. Then pain throws me to sitting, and I rock and moan, still almost asleep. The masseuse feels into my back and chest. I think the source is under my shoulder blade. She thinks it's more anterior. Our analysis, as inconclusive as it is, soothes me.

I increase my regular fistfuls of anti-inflammatories to the limits of my liver. A physician prescribes a narcotic. The last time I took narcotics was decades ago, and I remember lying spent on the bathroom floor, skin like ice, my body shaking with nausea, and seeing dancing shadow people on the walls, but the doctor reassures me that this one is very mild. The first pill is lovely. After the second I don't hallucinate, but I'm in the bathroom, at the toilet, tilted sideways over my wheelchair. The bottle is still in my fridge, if you ever need a little something.

I remember that my mother has died. I have an inheritance. For the first time in these decades of adjustment, I have extra money. My home has accrued grime. Things are stacked in corners. I hire people to clean the blinds, put away the winter clothes, wash the bedding, change lightbulbs, and mow the lawn. That mattress I splurged on, it's now twenty years old. I replace it. The new one costs a stunning amount of money, but I sleep with less pain. I find a chiropractor to add to my mix of support. He's one of the ones with forms that ask you questions like "What has this experience taught you?" This can indicate someone creepy about disability, but he laughs when he reads my answer ("That pain sucks"), so I figure we're going to be fine. The night after his third treatment, I wake up thinking that the moon is very bright through the window shades. It's the sun. I've slept through till morning, and the relief of it makes all things seem possible. The next night is rough again, but I've acquired hope. There is still a place, inside my mind, where my arm is okay.

It takes only a little hope for the fear to settle. I can think again. I make changes in my daily life. I pause and arrange my body for the smoothest transfer rather than just tossing myself at the bed or chair or toilet. I stop throwing open doors with a stiff arm held out in front of me. Instead I ask for help. Asking for help and especially the waiting for help annoy me. This carefulness with what were once deft movements annoys me. I use more of the dead mother money to fence the back yard, and now I don't have to walk the dog as often. I teach her to close the door behind her. I taught her long ago to pick up dropped keys, pens, papers, and even small books off the floor and place them in my lap, but now it's worth my while to wait for her to do it. My arm improves. I sleep four hours at a time routinely. I lift glasses of water, although I always do a test squeeze first. As my arm hurts less, I add more, and then my arm hurts more, and then I back off, and then I push again to the edge.

I have a dinner party. I know what you're thinking, but I needed one. Planning the menu is the most fun I've had in a while. The final decision is to go with bacon-wrapped scallops on the grill. With a few days' work, the table is set and glamorous. I can fit five around it, so I invite two couples—a set of old friends and one of new. The new ones already have a ramp to their house and even an accessible bathroom so anything is possible, friendship-wise. My old friends have an understanding of how much it took to open the door to them, offer an appetizer of steamed asparagus and yogurt dip seasoned with dill clipped from a pot hanging off my ramp, and say, "I need to check the grill, I'll be right back." The new ones don't. There's pleasure in being both known and unknown. Although over the dessert of vanilla ice cream, sliced strawberries, and the optional grating of nutmeg, among the conversations about our day, it comes up that the new couple almost canceled at the last moment. Not for any big reason. They had just spent too much time on errands during the day. My long-term friends both look over the table to meet my eyes. It embarrasses me that they know how much of a heartbreak that would have been. I turn my head to dip a spoon decorated with the royal Tudor crest into what used to be a cup to hold soft-boiled eggs. It's filled with minced lemon balm cut from another of the herb pots on my porch. "I thought this might go well with the ice cream. Does anyone else want to give it a try?"

This may be my last dinner party. I've lost too much writing time to it. But yes, I keep kayaking, although more and more before each trip, I brace against the thought of how much I'll hurt later. I pay more attention to the tide schedule and wind speeds, but no matter what, for three days after, I move in slow motion as each muscle I use declares itself in a rising up of pain. I sit and watch television in a blur of fatigue. Still, so far, it's worth it. I paddle through a salt marsh that smells like the origin of life itself, and the glory of it is not yet an illusion, a memory. It's still real in the moment, and I've learned that in the moment and forever are the same thing.

Horror in the Okefenokee

Six hours of paddling and a chilly day for South Georgia mean the only reason I know my backside is there is because it always has been. I'm back in the Okefenokee, but I have my own kayak now. There was no one to stop me from getting out on the water, no one to caution me about the cold. Can you get frostbite on your butt? I decide you can't but am imagining a hot shower as I paddle out of the swamp and up the canal to the marina. My wheelchair still stands sentinel at the boat ramp.

I wedge the kayak between the uneven cinder blocks at the bottom of the ramp. Now all I have to do is my usual: roll out of the boat, scooch over the concrete, balance on all fours, rise onto my knees, and twist into the seat of my wheelchair. At least the cold means no one is hanging out by the water. Besides the way people act funny when I crawl by, an observer always makes something go awry—like losing my shoes or trapping one breast under the seat on my way up.

Before I can start my roll over the side, a ranger bundled up in an overcoat and gloves appears at the top of the ramp. He's not the one from years ago. He chats about the weather. He asks about my trip. How many alligators? Any otters? He lingers. Knees to chest, arms clasped around them to stop the shivering, I try to wait him out. He keeps talking. He is immune to my mental cursing. In the middle of his story about the year it snowed, I abandon modesty and make my moves. More than once, I am butt-first in his direction.

Panting and finally sitting face forward in my chair, I smile at the ranger. I'm pleased at my accomplishment. His neck and face are sweaty and red. His expression is professionally bland, but I can see the horror underneath. Eyes averted, he mutters something and rushes away, disappearing over the top of the ramp. This pisses me off. So what that I don't move the way he does. Why can't people just deal with, admire even, someone figuring out how to do whatever it is they want to do? Why doesn't he appreciate my skill, my ingenuity, my enthusiasm? And now he's run off right when I could use some help hauling the kayak up the ramp.

It isn't until I'm at my campsite, blood returning to my backside, that I feel something cold and bare. Have I mentioned that I don't use underwear while kayaking? It gets wet. It bunches. Squirming from side to side, I strip off the thread-worn, used-only-for-kayaking pants. I hold them in front of me. Except for three frayed strips of material, the seat is gone. That last trip along the concrete was too much for it. I had been left exposed. I picture my pasty-white-with-cold cheeks pointed at the ranger with the ragged remains of the pants stretched across them looking not unlike a balding man's bad comb-over.

To my disappointment, I can't stay mad about the guy's sweaty, abrupt departure, and I mentally apologize for my unwarranted and unkind thoughts. As it turns out, big, naked butt cheeks waving around were what made him leave. If I'd mooned him right away, I realize, I'd be less cold now. I save the pants.

I'm Fine, Thank You

After another kayak trip, after my muscles recoup and my brain works again, I try to think ahead. This way I'll already have thought ahead if (when) another big change is needed, and I can keep being out on the water. But what could that change be? Would a new backrest or new type of cushion help? Perhaps a wheelchair that tilts, which would be like carrying my own hammock along with me. The absurdist year of full-time struggle it took to wrench this last wheelchair out from the medical establishment is remembered in a posttraumatic way. I don't know whether I have enough fight in me to do that again. I'll just have to use my arm less. How much less?

I start at my grocery store. These are people I don't really know and who have always wanted to help more than I allow. Now I let them lift the filled grocery bag and hang it by its cloth straps on the back of my wheelchair. When they don't offer, I ask them to do it. After I've practiced this with strangers, I move on to friends. "I'm not opening doors anymore," I announce. And sometimes I remember to stop, pull to the side, and wait for a companion to come around. For the most part, friends are adjusting. I'm adjusting. But arm pain can still control my day, my mind.

I'm awarded a writing fellowship and travel to a place I've never been before and where no one knows me. Before I go, I'm asked about what I plan to accomplish, and I talk of essays and a novel. I don't share my other plan. This will be a test. In a place where food is provided, there's no dog to care for, my room is cleaned, my sheets are changed, and no one requires anything of me, I'll find out if and how much my arm can improve in six weeks. No one will know me there. They will not know what I can and can't do or what I usually do for myself.

Once I'm there, over and over, I say I can't. I can't move the antique, high-backed chair away from the dining table. I can't help with the chopping for a party bowl of sangria. I can't lift the fan. It seems dishonest. I mean, I could do these things. I do carry my own plates back to the kitchen as all good residents do. They're heavy and sometimes I have to wait, holding them, in a crowd around the counter, and the pain creeps into my muscles. They would have done it for me, if I'd never started doing it, but now it feels too late. I can make only so many changes at once, even with people who wouldn't know they were changes.

For a month my arm does well. Then it hurts more. Then more. I slip away from evening parlor games and into the shadow of an alcove and perch beside the marble busts of dead people and hold my arm and pant and moan. Perhaps if anyone wanders by, I'll be taken for one of the resident ghosts. I also call around for acupuncturists and chiropractors in the area. I don't know why I thought I could skip all this for six weeks and not have consequences. I hate these new dependencies. And my experiment has failed. Even with housekeepers and cooks and no daily responsibilities, my arm is not back to regular, whatever that was. "Danger ahead" screams out of the ancient part of my brain.

I make myself think about a hypothetical future. I know people who don't transfer out of their wheelchairs on their own. They have jobs and loved ones and do important work. They have fun.

They travel the world. They make their own decisions. They hire people to get them up in the morning, bathe them, dress them, handle their toilet needs, put them to bed at night. I tally up my dead mother money. It's more than I've ever had, but I should be careful not to change my carefulness with money. I will need it. Just in case.

None of this soothes me, but I understand why friends haven't always embraced what seemed to me sage advice or been comforted by what I considered my successes. And the people who, throughout my life, have viewed me only as a nightmare version of a possible future, I still spit on their limited and ignorant minds. But for the first time, I recognize a part of myself in them. It is in this spirit that I decide I'm transferring fine. It just hurts a little more than it used to. Even as I conclude that there's no need to think ahead to something that might never happen, I know I'm like these people I've scorned, the people who think they're not headed for change. And I respect their fear more. I better understand the practicality of dishonesty. Bucking up is not always useful, and I'm weary of circumspection.

The Blind Girl and the Cripple Get on a Plane

For the first time in twenty years, I'm boarding a plane. I'm spending two thousand dollars on a trip for no good reason, for fun. The boarding chair hasn't changed. It's still a narrow ledge of a seat welded onto a dolly. I slide over from my wheelchair and perch on top of it. Burly guys crisscross my body with straps and tie me in. They say to fold my arms over my chest. They check one last time, cinch the strap over my bosom tighter and then tip the chair backward onto its wheels. I stare at the acoustic tiles. Remember that scene in *Silence of the Lambs* when Hannibal Lecter is rolled out over the tarmac? All I'm missing is the mask. A guy behind me, a guy at my feet, they bump me over the lip from walkway to plane. I make a joke about fava beans and a nice Chianti, but they don't get it. Beckie leans over me, so that I can see her face. I flick my tongue at her. She gets it.

Beckie is carrying all the parts we can possibly detach from the wheelchair. I've heard the horror stories of what happens once they whisk the chair away to be loaded into the belly of the plane. She has the footrests dangling from her arms and the $300 cushion hanging from one hand. Most important of all, the joystick controller is bubble wrapped and pinned under her elbow.

I'm jerked past the stewardesses, around a corner, and pulled backward down an aisle about as wide as an egg noodle. I don't remember it being this pinched. Even strapped tight, my thighs slide and catch against armrests. If I look down through my chest and beyond my footman, I can see Beckie following. She has to shuffle sideways because of her wide load, but she's doing fine. We can't let the airlines know she's legally blind in case our seats end up near the emergency exit. They'd make us move—as if a woman who knows how to negotiate in a smoky, blacked-out environment is not exactly who you'd want to be feeling around for the release levers. Today, we're deep into the plane. They don't seem to care what would happen to me sitting so far away from an exit.

The guys tilt me upright. I wave them off as they start to unstrap me and do it myself. After coming through security ("And when I touch the more personal areas I will use the back of my hand"), I need a break from strange hands all over my body. Beckie is scanning for the seat numbers. She doesn't have much peripheral vision, but it's plenty light so that helps.

"Look at a headrest and then look straight up." I murmur it.

Beckie nods, finds our numbers, and loads wheelchair gear into the overhead carrier. I don't have a good view of the seats, but as I've been warned, they've become much narrower. At least there will be just the two of us in the row. Beckie turns, and I get a better view. There are three seats. I sort of yell at Beckie that she and her fellow flying customers have been frogs in a two-decades-long heating pot of shrinking seats. Why hadn't they done something? Beckie extends an arm over our seats and bows.

"Middle or aisle, Hannibal?"

My friends travel. They go to Barcelona, China, New Zealand, Taiwan, and Brazil. Me, too, I thought. Before I had to use my savings for a new roof or some unexpected surgery, I would travel.

I spend hours researching all the European cities that had hosted the Paralympics. Usually they are the ones with the best accessibility. Barcelona seems perfect. But for the first time in my life, I'm scared to go by myself. Or maybe I'm not scared—maybe traveling with another person is just good sense and the only way I'll be relaxed enough to have fun. I don't have to figure this out because my friend Beckie calls and says, "Let's go somewhere."

We've planned this trip as if it were a Mars landing. It takes months. Barcelona is too much for Beckie. We research Vancouver, and I'm awash in websites about bookstores, art, food, good accessibility, and a whole different geography. I renew my passport. Beckie suggests that two plane transfers are too many for my first trip. How about Santa Fe? She'll figure out the flight and shuttles. I'll figure out the accommodations and all the nonplane travel. We call each other most days. We have strategy lunches. Both of us know that to make sure every part of the journey is wheelchair accessible we have to contact each place twice, talk to a different person each time to make sure the information matches, and get it in writing. The plane is cheaper on the weekend, hotels during the week. But the connecting city bus and train have different schedules on the weekend. I decide that my mother's money can help us pay for a fancier, more centrally located hotel. Each decision limits other choices, and we run scenarios. If that doesn't work, we revise a different, earlier decision. One day we find a scenario that runs all the way through. Beckie rechecks all the flight times. I look up all the train and bus schedules one more time. When Beckie presses the buy button on the tickets, and I make the hotel reservations, we both almost cry from the relief. And we're proud. We're a team. We figured it out.

We have back-up plans for everything. Except the wheelchair. It has to survive the trip or we're screwed. We go to my repair shop together, and they show us how to unplug and detach controls. I get a copy of the government pamphlet for the "Air Traveler with a Disability," which lists all my rights. I plan to wave it around if needed. I talk to a friend who travels with a power chair exactly like mine. She's casual and cavalier about everything. I can't relate. I go back to the repair place and buy extra caster bearings and get more tie straps. I write and laminate handling instructions for the ground crew and figure out where to attach them on the back of the wheelchair. Later I'm told that they should have been in Spanish.

But that's all done now. We're in the execution phase. And we've already survived our first glitch. The driver of the airport parking lot shuttle had no idea how to work the wheelchair lift. While we waited for a supervisor, we were relaxed and smug about having built in a two-hour leeway. Did we know how to do this or what?

Beckie pulls out her bag of trail mix, gets her earbuds ready, and sets her iPhone to the latest "This American Life" podcast. I'd shopped the airport bookstore before we boarded. *The Girl with the Dragon Tattoo* seemed like airplane reading the best I could figure. It balances on my lap as I lean over to position the wheelchair backpack under my feet to keep them from dangling. It hurts my hips when they dangle. The other two hundred and seventy passengers brush past, and their carry bags flop onto my shoulder. I wince each time another bag is shoved over my head. I imagine it slamming against the electronic controls of my wheelchair and worry that four layers of bubble wrap aren't enough. Everyone squirms and settles into their assigned slots.

The doors are closed. The stewardess tells me I have to put the pack underneath me. The engines suck in air, and I'm pushed against my seat. I remember this part. The g-forces subside and we're in flight.

Green and gray clouds roll along the shoulders of the mountains and make an early night on one side of us. We're standing on a sidewalk in Santa Fe. On the other side is such a blue sky. We don't have this blue in Florida. Lightning snaps over the mountains. Mountains. A splatter of rain falls and then stops.

Beckie walks at my side, a little behind, holding on to the handle of my wheelchair. I'm like a sailor standing the watch, ready to call out the dangers ahead as the ship of my wheelchair motors down the sidewalks. Only instead of rocky shoals or enemy ships, it's crumbled concrete and fire hydrants and elevation changes as we drop down curb cuts or cross driveways.

"How about the O'Keeffe museum tomorrow? I'm moving right to miss that pole."

Beckie and I do our side swerve move.

"How about lunch at that . . ."

"Down dip." I interrupt as my front caster wheels twist into a driveway drop. Beckie can usually tell just by feeling the wheelchair shift, but it never hurts to say it.

". . . place with the courtyard?"

"Up dip. And I want to go to the poetry reading at the bookstore tomorrow. I have to crowd you to the left."

Beckie and I do a coordinated side swerve. She compliments me on getting my left and rights right. All my life I've mostly switched them. More than once I've directed Beckie into an obstacle instead of away from it. But it's been better lately.

"Those dog obedience classes, you know. It helps."

Beckie barks. We laugh. I'm flopping over a stretch of broken concrete before I can say anything, but Beckie hears me groan as my hips jerk. She knows what that means and minces her steps. The next corner is a crisscross of guide wires and concrete pillars.

"We're coming up on a bunch of crap. Just get behind me." And now I'm Beckie's seeing-eye wheelchair. I weave through the obstacles. People always think she's pushing me.

There's enough rain now that we escape into the first open shop. It's a gallery of Russian art. It's still the same day I left Florida and already I've traveled through the backyards of pueblos with their beehive hornos and seen basalt-capped mountains, cottonwood trees, and yellow sprays of snakeroot. On the train we met a woman who studies the archaeology of outer space. For real. She has a contract with NASA. And now this, mosaic pieces of birch bark wood by someone whose name I remember as Ivan Ivanovich.

It's stopped raining. Beckie and I recheck the name of the restaurant the hotel gave us. It's just at the top of the street, they said. We keep walking. I'm stupid tired. I wouldn't trust myself to drive, but all I have to do is find the sign for the restaurant. Lightning outlines the shape of the mountains. Today the mountains we flew over looked small, but the pilot said ten thousand feet high. Later, through the big window of the train, I thought I saw a volcano. The outer space archaeologist looked at me funny and said, "No, that's a hill maybe a hundred feet high." My eyes are still set on Florida landscapes. They don't know how to focus to the extremes.

"Damn it, Sandra."

I've clipped Beckie's ankle with an unannounced turn to the left. Besides the left right mix-ups, my tendency to wander in my mind can be a problem. I watch Beckie rub her knee. Another bruise I've caused. I look for the restaurant. It should be right here. We probably went by it while I pondered elevation and eye muscles. We head back down the hill. I'm not used to hills. The wheelchair stops and starts differently, and my legs already ache from straining to push myself back in the chair. Uphill is easier. We should have seen the restaurant by now. I stop and ask. He points to right where we were. And there it is. I lead Beckie back.

"Isn't this right where we were?"

Sometimes Beckie sees things just fine.

The water out of the faucet is like liquid ice. It reminds me of Norway and tightens the tiredness out from under my eyes as well as any facial. The night before, at the restaurant we finally found, the smells of unknown spices floated through the air. My skin is still coated with them. I leave a note and let myself out of the hotel room where, even through my sunglasses, the glare of sun, its dryness, pulls at my eyes.

I wander the city beyond where we ate last night. Each time I touch my joystick, I'm traveling over ground new to me. The bookstore is open even at nine in the morning, and it's huge and intelligently stocked, and the staff is friendly and helpful, and I leave with *The Land of Little Rain*, essays written in 1903 by a woman who has abandoned her husband and child to live here in Santa Fe. I find the Indian Market. I travel along the line of blankets and watch down at my wheels to make sure I don't run over any bracelets, earrings, Christmas ornaments, pottery, or, to my delight, bookmarks made of copper and inlaid with turquoise. I see a bracelet of interlinking silver chains. I ask the price, and it's $300. I move on, but I'm calculating. On one blanket, just laid out there in the open, no security other than the long, side-by-side community of merchants, sits many thousands of dollars' worth of merchandise. The old store manager in me is stunned.

Every new image seen, item touched, and way of being considered does something good inside my body. Although this airiness in my bones could be from the elevation. I drink more water, as they say to. Later Beckie and I drink Mesoamerican chocolate elixirs whose ingredients are duplicated from DNA swabbed out of ancient Mayan ceremonial bowls. We laugh at the affectedness of it all, but we'll be back. We go to the Native American Contemporary Art Museum, where a massive, reclining woman sculpted of mud and sticks rises out of the floor. I stand in front of an iron whirligig of a sculpture twenty feet high, whose flickers and twirls make me clap my hands and laugh like a child. We tour a cathedral filled with the devout. My absence of belief seems intrusive, so I leave. Each time I look up, there are mountains. Each time, it's a surprise. And no matter how long I'm up in my wheelchair, my ankles don't swell. I twist my head from side to side in the mirror to admire new earrings and see how the dryness has etched the lines of my face into a darker relief. And under the necklaces I try on, my chest has become a draping of wrinkles. My whole body is different here. One day I go back to the hotel room because of nausea and an unexpected wash of tiredness. I know these are the symptoms of altitude sickness. I force down as much water as I can and pass out for the rest of the day and into the night. The next morning I'm fine.

The mountains have changed in my fifteen hours of seclusion. I worry about the spreading yellow patches—are there swathes of trees dying? I don't say anything to Beckie. I don't want to know about the pollution or mining or whatever travesty it might be.

April, a friend of a friend, comes to take us out of the city. She points right at the damaged areas on the slopes and talks about how gorgeous it is each fall as the aspen trees change colors.

April drives us into the high desert. She's a geologist. She points at huge landscapes folded by heat and pressure when the land was deep underground and then to fanned skirts of rock sculpted by the surface forces of water. There, there, she almost shouts, are the remains of a shield volcano. She teaches us about colors, that red equals iron oxide. April talks of how she has come to see colors differently. I think she means the way the monotone of beige rocks brightens into fuchsias and lemons the more you stare. But she speaks of the bright paint on houses, the combinations of purple and turquoise, the change in her personal aesthetic away from the Southern California suburbs of her childhood. And anyway, she says, the sun fades everything. You have to start out bright.

The road is now sliced into a cliff. April throws her hand up to the windshield. "Look, look, that line way up there of gray, sort of green, above the red. It's called *gley*. That's where, oh, hold on." The car swerves off to the side of the road. We idle on the verge while April takes a breath and explains. The gray area is the same as the red area above, but the gray, over a long time, has had all the minerals dissolved out of it and into the rock below. This could happen only from water. She keeps looking over at us as if we're supposed to at some point get it, understand, join in her excitement. We look up at the wall of rock. It's rock. April reaches the great reveal of her story. "Which is how you know that way up there was the very bottom of a swamp." It's as if a loved one has appeared unexpectedly. My arms fling out. A swamp. I know swamps. I ignore the passage of eons and feel the ancient waters surround me. They aren't lapping over me or rocking a boat under my thighs as in Florida, but for the first time these massive landscapes are more than just observed. A part of them is inside me.

April has borrowed an old manual wheelchair. It's folded and in the back of the suv. It's rude, but I slap the dashboard and demand to be let out of the car. April says to wait. She'll find a safer place. She finds what might be a long driveway to someone's unseen house. We drive a quarter mile on the gravel, and April stops. First, she says, she has to check whether her tires have shredded. Is this a thing that might happen?

Beckie goes to help her lift the wheelchair out of the back. She shows April how to flip the sides apart. I do a long transfer down to the old hospital clunker that's too heavy for me to push on my own more than a few feet. Beckie rolls me some twenty yards over the parched red dirt that slides under the wheels. We reach areas of graveled earth, and here the wheels dip and strain. We pass cactus as big as trees and leafed yucca plants. We disturb a scurry of ants. A pile of dumped trash is pierced through by stalks of purple-flowered grasses. I tell Beckie that this is far enough. She wanders off behind me, and I twist in the chair to look ahead of her path to check for dangers. Could there be a sudden crevasse? An old mine shaft? This terrain is unknown to me. Nothing obvious is visible, and so I turn front in the wheelchair again, slump into the sling back and close my eyes. I hear wind and then feel it. I hear the silence of large spaces. I open my eyes and try to understand the relative depths of grottos, the heights of rocks. April has walked into the hills. She disappears and reappears and returns with flakes of chert and quartz and iron. She's happy. We take pictures of the various configurations of us in pairs.

I find a way on the map that takes us over the mountains to home. We drive to where the sign warns us of a dangerous road. April says no way and turns around and goes to find a freeway. There a car races past us, pulls into the exit lane, pulls back, slides to the outside lane, and scrapes along the concrete divider in a spray of sparks. We and the other cars slow, and the impaired driver becomes the drum major of a band of cars following behind until a police car sirens by on the inside emergency lane. By the time we pass, they have cut in front of the car. A young, pale man is rolling on the ground, handcuffed. The officer puts a hand under his arm and lifts him like a package. She is built solid, with a brown, sun-etched face and a black braid down her back.

Beckie and I encourage April to stop at a roadside diner that promises homemade pies. We have tamales, which April rates as very good. At the next table a group of old men entertain each other with stories about women and land deals and trucks. At one point the voices drop, and my eavesdropping is useless until one of them reaches his punch line. "And that's when about five types of law showed up." The whole restaurant laughs along with them. April drops us at the hotel. Without her, her driving, the wheelchair, we never would have left the city. The claustrophobia of how that would have been makes me thank April again and again. She leaves to go back to her nearby home. I'm ready for more pain meds. I take them and go to bed. When I wake up, I hurt, and I am also contented.

My routine becomes to go to the bookstore in the mornings. They know me by name now. Beckie usually goes for a long walk first thing. One day I'm bringing a blueberry muffin back to Beckie, and there she is walking my way. She opens the bag and eats and talks, crumbs flying. She's had an adventure. She followed a sidewalk west out of town, through neighborhoods until it became a rough trail over hills. She walked uphill from rise to just one more rise until she remembered April saying they had rattlesnakes and bears in their back yard, so she turned around. She went down the graveled, slick, tilted, narrow path without any falls. There was just that once she'd almost grabbed a cactus to support herself. We talked about what was considered foolish or irresponsible of us by our friends and family. How we, in turn, enjoyed horrifying them. And how much the whole idea of adventure had changed, especially for children. How Beckie's mother had let her batch of kids roam the woods near the house, where they climbed trees hundreds of feet high.

This was the day we were going to the Georgia O'Keeffe museum. It was a perfect museum, small and intimate with a devoted staff. We wandered the seven gallery rooms and then did it all over again when the crowd thinned. Now we could place ourselves far away from the landscapes, and they became more: fuller, dimensional, and—paradoxically—increasingly detailed. How had she done that? She couldn't have been more than her own arm's length away while she painted them. And there was the flat, bread-loaf shape of a mountain I had seen on our drive. With my own eyes, I couldn't make it seem more than two-dimensional, but here, on a flat sheet of canvas, I saw the immensity and into the folded depths.

The outer space archaeologist had told us to eat at the Shed. There is a line, so we wait in the courtyard garden alongside a daughter about my age and her mother. I slide my wheelchair in alongside the mother's. I smile at her. She stares off into some far place. The daughter takes her mother's hand and says, "She left this consciousness a while back." Then she holds the straw of a margarita close enough to brush her mother's lips. The lips open and suck and let go. The old woman smiles all the way up to her eyes. Her daughter says, "Happy birthday, Mom." I say that my mother has died, and then our buzzer goes off. I lean over my armrest and look into the woman's vague face. I wish her happy birthday. She smiles again.

At the table, Beckie and I toast to Yvonne, my mother, before we eat green chili soup and enchiladas with both green and red chili, one sharp and exciting and the other velvet smooth. The pinto beans still have sunshine in them. We eat too much and have to refuse their famous mocha cake.

April comes again and drives us into the mountain, into the aspens. Their leaves are orange and red and all the yellows. They flicker like coins in the wind. We climb and leave the aspens behind, and firs, Christmas tree firs, step up the mountainside. At curves we look down on folds of gold and green topped by blue, no-humidity blue, with white clouds moving fast. The air becomes cold. Rocks are tumbled alongside the road.

There's a ski lift at the top. I get into the old wheelchair and make Beckie push me closer until I can see that I could get on. A sign promises us 11,250 feet of elevation. April looks at my face and goes to buy our fares. She comes back with just two tickets because she's scared of heights. I don't even pretend to protest. When Beckie and I get loaded onto the seat and it rises and rocks so that I grip the bar with one hand and the back of the seat with the other, I remember that I'm scared of heights as well. It's too late to stop, and I'm glad. We go so high, both from the ground and up the mountain. Each time the lift stops, and wires groan, I grip harder. Pain is settling into my shoulder. I shake my fingers loose until the next groan. We reach the top, are circled around, and now as we descend, the vista is in front of us. It's cold. My teeth chatter. The treetops are under our feet. The sunlight travels over the mountainside in front of us and changes the colors the way it does over Florida prairies.

The seat rocks and stutters, and we tilt face-forward into a long drop to the rocks over and over again. I decide that all my strength won't prevent the line snapping or hold us if we dangle from a broken seat, so I manage to let go of the armrest. I even take pictures, which means neither hand is holding on to anything. Closer to the end, we see people climbing below us. And we see April bent over, looking for rocks. She waves. At the bottom, when we meet up again, she says that as we took off she thought, "I've lost my chance." I say to her, a little unctuously, maybe more than a little, that there's always another chance. My excuse is that really, I'm saying it to myself. April gives me quartz with mica and explains how the mica formed in pours, how the lighter quartz oozed over and into it and hardened. She says this quartz has micro crystals. If it had cooled more slowly, it would have become a geode with large crystals inside.

The last morning of our trip, I'm sure my dog has died. I can't reach my friends who are taking care of her. I decide they're avoiding my calls, so they won't have to tell me. The grief is overwhelming. Finally they answer. The dog is fine. I sleep all afternoon and wake up groggy, so I watch *Bones* reruns. Beckie is off wandering. Through a crack in the hotel curtains, I notice that the light is fading, so I get dressed and go outside, only to return and put on the heaviest sweater that I've packed. The weather, the season, is changing. I wander the streets thinking I'll run into Beckie, but when the light turns that thick gray, I call her. She's around a corner, not a hundred feet from me, almost to the hotel, having timed her travels perfectly to be back before dark. We find each other, she swings around to my side to hold onto the wheelchair, and we make a last round of the city, past the lit-up cathedral where we put money in the box of a juggler who balances on an exercise ball and throws batons into the air. He says he likes to do it with machetes, but the city won't let him. We get a piece of mocha cake from the Shed and share it in their courtyard. We stop at a display window where an artist is advertising her gallery show. She calls it *Internalized Landscapes Remembered from Travels*. This is what I try to write, I think. "Beckie," I say, "this right here is worth the trip." We have time before the train the next afternoon, so I copy down the address of her gallery.

I finish packing early in the morning and have a last visit to the blanket market. I buy a bracelet. It costs $130. I'm inordinately pleased with this physical thing, and it is beautiful, but I know the pleasure comes also from having spent the money. Just like that. With no worry. With no calculation of the future. I follow my now split-at-the-creases city map to Canyon Road, where galleries line the street. The gallery I'm looking for turns out to have steps. What with the wild mood I'm in, this artist just lost out on a sale. I keep exploring, follow a driveway behind a building, and there, sweeping down in front of me, is a forest of the whirligig, wind-driven sculptures. I scream into the phone to Beckie that she must come and see.

The trip home is filled with all those things we worried about. A hotel lies about having an accessible room. I beat against the plane window as a ground crew slams my wheelchair onto its side. They can't hear me. The wheelchair is delivered to me with levers broken, and no one since 9/11 has a screwdriver, which is all it would take for me to jury-rig it into mobility. Finally an exception is made. A screwdriver is found, and we can leave the airport. Beckie and I are so tired that we miss an exit and add forty miles to our drive home. I don't care. I don't worry about how much I'll hurt tomorrow and the next day and the week after that. Instead I remember the taste of ancho chili chocolate elixir and the long view over outcrops of juniper and piñon.

The Swimmer

My friend Mary has surgery. She uses a power wheelchair the
same as me. For a while now, before going into the hospital,
she's lived in an assisted care center. After her surgery, she's put
in a room with no window, and for two weeks no natural light
falls over her body. She wants to die. She's been ready to die
for about a year now, but this is different. She's in despair. She
tells everyone who enters the room—the nurses, the doctors, the
women who mop the floor—that she wants to die.

Each time I visit Mary in the hospital, I prepare. I arm myself
with good food and magazines and prepared topics of conversation, and still I can hardly make myself get in the car. I circle
the hospital to look for a parking place and hope I won't find
one. I take deep breaths to offset a drowning panic. It's hard to
see Mary in this situation. It's hard because she's my friend,
and it's hard because I'm thinking of myself and what it would
be like for me. Mary has a daughter and her daughter's partner
who care for her in a daily, primary way. Mary has plenty of
money. Mary has excellent medical insurance.

On one visit, a nurse pulls me aside and asks if this is regular,
this wanting to die. I ask her if anyone has helped Mary brush
her teeth or wash her face this morning. I go into the room
and turn on all the lights. Mary complains, and I turn them
off, except for one. At least now the room is not in permanent
twilight. I've come with food Mary likes. She says she can't eat
anything. She just wants to die. She shuts her eyes. I bustle
around the room. I throw out scraps of alcohol wipes scattered

on her sheets. I throw out old water cups and straws and wipe smears of lotion off her bedside table. Her eighty-eighth birthday was two days ago. I rearrange all her cards and flowers around the room, so maybe the staff will notice her. I make as much noise as I can. I catch her looking at me. I offer her one of the lemon-poppy seed muffins I've brought. She says she just can't eat anything. I say that I'm hungry, and she won't mind if I eat, will she? I rustle the bags. She opens her eyes and watches me. She asks if that's the same chicken salad I brought before. I answer, from around a full mouth, that it is. She asks for some. I bring her a fork and the chicken salad, and soon we're eating together in a companionable way. We take turns exclaiming how good it is. I describe the little shop where I bought it and how it's just at the other end of the strip mall with the bookstore she likes to visit.

No one comes in to check on her. I ask if anyone has helped her brush her teeth. "No, no one. Not the whole time I've been here," she says. "They treat me like I'm already dead," she says. I'm never sure whether she has the facts right. Her sense of time got screwed up after the first week she was here. Still I'm angry. I can't fit on the side of her bed where her toiletries are. I can't reach to set her up with a basin and washcloth. I go into the hall to find someone and make them come help, but it's like a Stephen King novel out there. The halls are empty. The desk areas are empty. I can't hear anyone talking anywhere. I look in other rooms. There are just people in beds and machines beeping. I go back to Mary and offer her a muffin. "Yes, please," she says.

The day comes that Mary is discharged to rehab. We ask the hospital social worker whether medical transport will load Mary's wheelchair. She has no idea. She goes and finds out. Yes, they will. She goes out again. She comes back. She says she checked with the rehab center, and they don't allow any electric wheelchairs in their facility. "How can that be? That just can't even be legal." My voice roars out through the room. I lose all perspective on this being about Mary, not me, but Mary is now echoing me. How can she ever get back to her apartment if she doesn't learn how to get back in her wheelchair? I agree with her. Then I remember that it's my job to say calm things, to assure. We'll figure this out, I say. These first days it won't matter. They'll just be working on getting you stronger. Just think, you'll get to see the outside. Mary is more animated than she's been in weeks. She has not mentioned wanting to die since yesterday.

The preparations are made. I remind myself over and over not to freak out, not to make it about me. My job is to make things work for Mary. Her daughter and I arrive right behind the van that's transporting Mary. Her daughter does the talking with the administrator. I keep quiet. This is about Mary, I remind myself. But then the administrator brings up the wheelchair again and how it's not allowed. Mary's wheelchair. Not mine. For some reason, it seems just fine that I'm using an electric wheelchair. I can't stop myself. "How can it be legal to separate someone from their wheelchair?" I know I'm intruding on what is a really hard time for Mary's daughter, my dear friend, for whom I should be a stalwart rock of support. This is so inappropriate. The administrator is taken aback. "It certainly is legal," she huffs. "Many nursing homes have that rule."

Mary is settled into her new place, a double room with a woman who has the TV turned so loud that none of us can hear what the other is saying. But Mary says no problem, she'll just take out her hearing aids. The bed is by a big window. I unpack her clothes into the dresser, put out the framed photos, and arrange her plant in a patch of sunlight while her daughter talks to the staff. A nurse comes in and asks intelligent questions about Mary's medications and answers our questions thoroughly. It is a relief. I go into the physical therapy room with the mats and weights and bars and vinyl smells that work on me in the manner of a forgotten childhood home. I ask the physical therapists about what Mary should wear for her workouts. I do all this and feel good about doing it, and I'm liking the place more, and I'm thinking that Mary might really get back to her own apartment soon. At the same time, some alter me is screaming down the halls and looking for an escape. The silent echoes of fear bounce off the walls and flood into my brain. On the way out, as the sliding doors close behind us, I say to Mary's daughter. "We have to make sure they let her out of here." Mary's daughter pats my arm. She takes us for ice cream.

Mary is now back at her retirement community among her friends and caretakers. She lets them help her take showers and sometimes dress her. She sleeps more and remembers less. But she has regained, with adjustments, the pattern of her days. She just hosted her annual Christmas dinner. She invites all of us, her friends and family, and plans for extra seats because each year she notices other residents who are on their own and invites them to join us. This year her daughter and her daughter's partner bring flowers from their garden to decorate the long table. A friend, the oldest of us all at ninety-eight, has brought LED votive candles to set at each place setting. I bring party favors, English Crackers, my mother's tradition from when she used to be here at this table with us, and we pop them open and read the funny jokes inside and put on the paper hats. It occurs to me that Mary has figured out how to keep having dinner parties.

My arm is better. The injury lingers in the tenderness of my elbow, the light slaps along my neck, the occasional life-stopping grab of pain. It's become a ghost that moans from the shadows, rattles chains, and only occasionally throws a gargoyle off the roof at my head. I automatically and without shame move to the side and wait for doors to be opened. I'm also making secret adjustments. I devise excuses not to kayak as often the way I used to make excuses when eating out. "Damn, my schedule is too tight. How about a stroll out over the Prairie instead?" I notice acquaintances who own motor boats and wonder if they'd like to be friends with me.

Again, I imagine the needs of possible future limitations, but this time with more curiosity and less panic. Would an electric motor on my kayak just make things harder? What would it take to get a wheelchair that tilts? Am I ready to give up my hot baths for a roll-in shower? I imagine changes the best I can, but each time my palm lingers over a cellulose-laden, pregrated tub of tasteless Parmesan cheese, I tell myself that some changes are wrong no matter how practical. What is important? Hand-grated cheese, I say and laugh at myself. Although now each time I ask the question "What is important?," I have no choice but to include the dog in the answer. Adding another living, unpredictable being into my planned, budgeted life has turned out to make a wild sort of sense. And it doesn't hurt that if I choose to go looking for love, I'll be moving through the world with a dog trotting easily alongside my wheels. I've become part of an overall adorableness. I can work with that..

Still, I can sense the deep sadness that will come, and I can't yet see the other side of this, the part where something I couldn't even have imagined comes into my life, where beyond fear and shame there is a grace of some sort. Is it even possible anymore? Do I keep trust that it will happen again, as it has always happened? I look up the word *apocalypse*. Down past talk of trumpets, devouring fire, and abominations of desolation, they say the word originates in Greek. It means the "revelation of something hidden."

I'm part of a group kayaking on Florida's Santa Fe River. We're with a turtle expert. He and his student aren't in kayaks. They swim along beside us with wetsuits, flippers, and snorkels in a flaunting of stamina and strength. From time to time, head down, they churn a wake through mats of pennywort, pickerelweed, and tall rushes whose inflorescences shake over our heads. They dive, flippers pointed to the sky before they disappear under the water. We paddle in place until they break the surface gripping a red-bellied turtle or a peninsula cooter or shouting the story of a ferocious Florida softshell that got away.

I'm ahead of everyone when the turtle guy stops to give an impromptu lecture. My kayak fits into a bit of shore between cypress trees. It's a Florida-hot day. The river water promises to be cool, so I roll over the edge of the boat and fall into the shallows. I make calculations. It's downstream to where the other people are. I'm not alone. If I can't make it back to my kayak, I'll hitch a tow. My hands set into the muck underneath me, and with one long pull I'm launched into the current.

My arms remember the flat arc of the stretch, my shoulder lifts forward, and my hands angle though the water without a splash. Over and over, my mouth tilts into the pocket of air scooped low alongside my head. The remembered rhythm moves through me, moves me through the water. From underground springs the cold water rushes along my stretched-out spine. I imagine a wake behind me, the turtles underneath me. My head hits against the plastic keel of a kayak. I've arrived. I dip under and around boats until I find a perch on a downed palm tree trunk.

The turtle guy is telling us how we are, right now, on this particular stretch of river, in a unique place in the world. Nowhere else has this diversity of species. He holds up turtles and shows us how this black stripe, those circles, that bowing of the shell tells us sex, age, how fast they swim. He passes them around. We feel the softness of their long claws, the strength of their carapaces. He bounces on his flippers as he says more than once, "And you know what the really cool thing is?"

I'm panting. I tilt, unbalanced, until I grip onto a friend's kayak for support. She puts a hand on my shoulder. When we're ready to move on, I push off the tree trunk and swim into the open. My arms find a slow rhythm against the current. Out in the center of the river I stop and let momentum fall away. Sunlight bends into the clear water and shines against my legs and the grasses underneath me. I exhale until I drop under the surface. The twist and flow of water rising from deep limestone caverns turns my body in slow circles. I can already feel the ache in my arms. Tomorrow, the next day, for the next week, I'll hurt from this. Today, however, I know who I am.

Rebecca Lindenberg's "Versus" originally appeared in *Love, an Index* (San Francisco: McSweeney's, 2012).

"Solace: Three of the Places" originally appeared in *Pithead Chapel* 5, no. 6 (2016).

"The Laundromat" originally appeared in *Lavandería: A Mixed Load of Women, Wash, and Word*, ed. Donna J. Watson, Michelle Sierra, and Lucia Gbaya-Kanga (San Diego: City Works Press, 2009). It later appeared in *Hippocampus Magazine* (June 2016) and again in *Selected Memories: Five Years of Hippocampus Magazine*, ed. Donna Talarico (Lancaster: Hippocampus Magazine and Books, 2017).

"Sex Objects" originally appeared in *Brevity* 49 (May 2015).

"Rolling in the Mud" was first published in *Alaska Quarterly Review* 22, nos. 1–2 (Spring and Summer 2011). It later appeared in *Hippocampus Magazine* (June 2015) and in *Not Somewhere Else but Here: A Contemporary Anthology of Women and Place*, ed. Erin Elizabeth Smith, T. A. Noonan, and Rhonda Lott (Knoxville: Sundress Publications, 2014).

"Poster Children" originally appeared in *Brevity* 46 (May 2014).

"Mosquitoes" originally appeared in DIAGRAM 15, no. 6 (2015).

"May or May Not" originally appeared in *New Letters* 79, no. 2 (Winter 2013) and later appeared in *Redux* #193 (February 2016).

"The Last Period" originally appeared in *Midway Journal* 9, no. 1 (2015).

"Looking for the V" originally appeared in *Something to Declare: Good Lesbian Travel Writing,* ed. Gillian Kendall (Madison: University of Wisconsin Press, 2009). © 2009 by the Regents of the University of Wisconsin System. Reprinted courtesy of The University of Wisconsin Press.

"I Am Here, in This Morning Light" first appeared in the *North American Review* 297, no. 4 (Fall 2012) and later appeared in *Best Women's Travel Writing Volume 11,* ed. Lavinia Spalding (Palo Alto: Travelers' Tales, 2017).

"Horror in the Okefenokee" originally appeared in *Breath and Shadow: A Journal of Disability Culture and Literature* (September 2007).

"The Blind Girl and the Cripple Get on a Plane" originally appeared in *Human Parts/Medium* on April 28, 2015.

"Etymology" originally appeared in the *Southern Review* (Spring 2017).

"A Certain Loneliness" originally appeared in *Water~Stone Review* 17 (2014–15).

"Atlanta—1968," "Atlanta—1984," and "Atlanta—2007" originally appeared together as "Sears Building Triptych" in *Atticus Review* (April 2015).

"Who I Am" originally appeared in *Arts & Letters* 27 (Spring 2013).

IN THE AMERICAN LIVES SERIES

Fault Line
by Laurie Alberts

Pieces from Life's Crazy Quilt
by Marvin V. Arnett

Songs from the Black Chair:
A Memoir of Mental Illness
by Charles Barber

This Is Not the Ivy League:
A Memoir
by Mary Clearman Blew

Body Geographic
by Barrie Jean Borich

Driving with Dvořák: Essays
on Memory and Identity
by Fleda Brown

Searching for Tamsen Donner
by Gabrielle Burton

Island of Bones: Essays
by Joy Castro

American Lives: A Reader
edited by Alicia Christensen
introduced by Tobias Wolff

Get Me Through Tomorrow:
A Sister's Memoir of Brain
Injury and Revival
by Mojie Crigler

Should I Still Wish: A Memoir
by John W. Evans

Out of Joint: A Private and
Public Story of Arthritis
by Mary Felstiner

Descanso for My Father:
Fragments of a Life
by Harrison Candelaria Fletcher

My Wife Wants You to Know
I'm Happily Married
by Joey Franklin

Weeds: A Farm
Daughter's Lament
by Evelyn I. Funda

Falling Room
by Eli Hastings

Opa Nobody
by Sonya Huber

Pain Woman Takes Your Keys,
and Other Essays from
a Nervous System
by Sonya Huber

Hannah and the Mountain: Notes
toward a Wilderness Fatherhood
by Jonathan Johnson

Local Wonders: Seasons
in the Bohemian Alps
by Ted Kooser

A Certain Loneliness: A Memoir
by Sandra Gail Lambert

Bigger than Life:
A Murder, a Memoir
by Dinah Lenney

What Becomes You
by Aaron Raz Link and Hilda Raz

Queen of the Fall: A Memoir
of Girls and Goddesses
by Sonja Livingston

Such a Life
by Lee Martin

Turning Bones
by Lee Martin

In Rooms of Memory: Essays
by Hilary Masters

Between Panic and Desire
by Dinty W. Moore

Sleep in Me
by Jon Pineda

The Solace of Stones: Finding a
Way through Wilderness
by Julie Riddle

Works Cited: An Alphabetical
Odyssey of Mayhem and
Misbehavior
by Brandon R. Schrand

Thoughts from a Queen-Sized Bed
by Mimi Schwartz

My Ruby Slippers:
The Road Back to Kansas
by Tracy Seeley

The Fortune Teller's Kiss
by Brenda Serotte

Gang of One:
Memoirs of a Red Guard
by Fan Shen

Just Breathe Normally
by Peggy Shumaker

Scraping By in the Big Eighties
by Natalia Rachel Singer

In the Shadow of Memory
by Floyd Skloot

Secret Frequencies:
A New York Education
by John Skoyles

The Days Are Gods
by Liz Stephens

Phantom Limb
by Janet Sternburg

Yellowstone Autumn: A Season of Discovery in a Wondrous Land
by W. D. Wetherell

When We Were Ghouls: A Memoir of Ghost Stories
by Amy E. Wallen

To order or obtain more information on these or other University of Nebraska Press titles, visit nebraskapress.unl.edu.